LITERATURE AND REVOLUTION

"CULTURAL SHIFTS: MODERNIST PERSIAN INFLUENCE ON 1979 IRAN"

DR. MD JAMSHED ALAM

INDIA • SINGAPORE • MALAYSIA

Made with ❤ on the Notion Press Platform
www.notionpress.com

Dedication:

"Dedicated to all who have fought to uphold and establish the right to freedom of expression."

Blurb

In "Literature and Revolution: Cultural Shifts: Modernist Persian Influence on 1979 Iran" explore how a wave of modernist thought in Persian literature helped shape the ideological and cultural currents leading to the Iranian Revolution of 1979. This book delves into the works of pioneering poets and writers who broke with tradition, embracing new forms and themes that resonated with a society amid profound change. Through their innovative use of language and exploration of contemporary issues, these literary figures not only reflected the discontent and aspirations of the Iranian people but also inspired a movement towards cultural and political transformation. "Literature and Revolution" uncovers the deep connections between art and societal upheaval, offering a nuanced understanding of how modernist literature influenced the revolutionary spirit of an era that redefined Iran's national identity.

Contents

Foreword

In the annals of world history, the 1979 Iranian Revolution stands as a seismic event that dramatically reshaped the political, social, and cultural landscape of Iran. While much has been written about the political and religious dimensions of this revolution, far less attention has been devoted to the profound cultural shifts that preceded and followed this transformative period. The intersection of literature and revolution is a compelling lens through which to understand the forces that both fueled and emerged from this historic upheaval.

This book, Literature and Revolution; Cultural Shifts: Modernist Persian Influence on 1979 Iran, seeks to explore the undercurrents of cultural transformation that played a crucial role in shaping the consciousness of a nation on the brink of change. At the heart of this exploration is the influence of Modernist Persian literature, a movement that, in its pursuit of new forms and expressions, both mirrored and challenged the evolving dynamics of Iranian society in the decades leading up to the revolution.

Modernist Persian literature was not merely a reflection of Western literary trends; it was a complex, indigenous response to the rapid modernization and Westernization of Iran under the Pahlavi dynasty. Writers and poets of this era, such as Sadegh Hedayat, Forugh Farrokhzad, and Nima Yooshij, grappled with themes of identity, alienation, and the tensions between tradition and modernity. Their works, characterized by innovation in language, form, and content, resonated deeply with a population increasingly disillusioned with the autocratic rule and the cultural policies imposed from above.

As this book will argue, the seeds of the 1979 revolution were sown not only in the political arenas but also in the literary and cultural fields. The Modernist Persian literary movement provided a critical space for intellectual and artistic dissent, where the complexities of Iranian identity could be interrogated, reimagined, and expressed in ways that would later inform the revolutionary ethos. The exploration of these cultural shifts offers a nuanced understanding of the revolution, revealing the intricate interplay between literature and the broader sociopolitical currents of the time.

In delving into the impact of Modernist Persian literature on the revolutionary consciousness, this book invites readers to reconsider the narratives of the 1979 Iranian Revolution. It challenges the notion that revolutions are driven solely by political ideologies, highlighting instead the significant role of cultural forces in shaping the course of history. Through this lens, we gain a deeper appreciation of the power of literature to not only reflect society but to actively participate in its transformation.

This foreword serves as an invitation to embark on a journey through the literary landscapes of pre-revolutionary Iran, where the modernist spirit thrived, and to uncover how these cultural shifts left an indelible mark on the revolution that would forever change the nation.

Prof (Dr) Zakira Sharif Qasmi

JNU.

Preface

Iran has always been a conspicuous case to discuss and bring into the academic discourse in central Asia. During the Reza Shah Pehlavi Iran had to struggle a lot to get basic rights like freedom and penetrate the democracy. The opposition against Reza Shah was at large because of his secret policy of implementing Savak to control the country. The opposition was mainly led by Khomeini, who was exiled to Iraq and later on to France. The progressive writers and activists also supported the idea of freeing Iran from the Shah. In January 1979, Shah left Iran and handed the country's command to Shapour Bakhtiar, who failed to manage the worst situation in Iran, and finally, civil war took place. In the month of April 1979, a national referendum took place, and Ayatollah Khomeini declared an Islamic republic with a new Constitution reflecting his ideals of Islamic government. The contribution of the literature (modern writing) style cannot be forgotten.

The first chapter deals with the socio-political conditions of Iran during the twentieth-century and specifically during the times of modern prose writers. It also deals with the rule of Reza Shah, the condition of the people during that time and the struggle for the Iranian revolution. A part of this chapter includes the elaboration on the role of a group of literary people who stood up against the deeds and arbitrariness of the Reza Shah regime. This chapter takes us to the arena of modernist writers who dared, challenged, and stood up against Reza Shah's rule.

The second chapter deals with how these modernist trends focus on revolutionary fiction, including the short story. These short stories are marked by dynamic experimentation with techniques of narration, choice of plot, imagery, and structure. The chapter also deals with the analytical study of Persian Literature in Iran. In line with recent tendencies in most modern literature, modern Persian fiction expresses doubts, uncertainty, anxiety, tension, paradox, and dilemmas. It tells of beginnings and not of ends. It deals with realism as a case in point of literature.

The third chapter takes into account the mainstream of the Iranian revolution following the major themes of that time reflected by modernist Persian literature. While the most important contribution of classic Persian literature in world literature is the most noteworthy among numerous literature historians and critics, the Persian-Iranian literature of the later period is generally disregarded. Short story writing takes its roots mainly from folklore tales and legends, ancient and classic forms of prose and storytelling, and then due to the contacts with the Arabic and European writing of the late nineteenth-century.

Finally, the Fourth Chapter talks about how the influence was done throughout the literary works by following and introducing the modern trend and approaches to short story writing in Iran by Jamalazadeh, Hedayat, Chubak, Bozorg Alvi, Jala Ale Ahmad, etc. This chapter broadly focuses on the mainstream impact generated by the writers of a new era. It also compares the nature, traits, and diverse forms of writing of these writers. This chapter goes into the details of the origin of short stories and the rationale behind these writings.

Acknowledgment

I would like to express my deepest appreciation and heartfelt thanks to my professors at Jawaharlal Nehru University New Delhi, Tata Institute of Social Sciencees, Mumbai, University of Tehran,Iran and University of Gothenburg, Sweden. You all have been an exceptional mentor, guiding me with wisdom and unwavering support. I am profoundly grateful for your encouragement in my research endeavors and for providing me with the opportunity to grow as a research scholar. Your invaluable advice, both in my academic journey and in life, has left a lasting impact on me.

I would also like to extend my sincere thanks to the faculty at my Centre for providing a nurturing academic environment, even during challenging times. Your support and understanding have been instrumental in helping me complete my research work. I am especially grateful for the freedom you have given me to think beyond conventional boundaries and for your insightful comments and suggestions.

I am deeply thankful to the University Grants Commission for awarding me the Dr. S. Radhakrishnan Post-Doctoral Fellowship. This book is a true reflection of the trust you have placed in my program, and I offer it as a token of my gratitude for your interest in my work.

A special thanks to my parents, my wife and my Brothers and sisters... words cannot fully capture how grateful I am for your love and support. Finally, I would like to thank my friends, who stood by me during this journey, encouraging me and inspiring me to strive toward my goals.

Introduction

This Book talks about the Literature and Revolution "CULTURAL SHIFTS: MODERNIST PERSIAN INFLUENCE ON 1979 IRAN". The Modernist Trend in Persian literature has had a great impact through the writing of various writers in Iran and abroad. Jamalzadeh is the first modern prose writer in Iran to portray and criticise the Reza Shah regime by depicting the real situation of Iran through his works. He was the first to introduce the European technique in Iran. His short story technique was not accepted by the people at large in the beginning. His stories were based on conversations between the characters using local dialects and foreign languages.

In the arena of the literary world, the modernist's pre-eminence is due mainly to their timely clarion call for a regeneration of Persian prose. The modernists seize every opportunity to quote maxims, poems, proverbs, and popular sayings, as well as Koranic verses and quotations from the traditions. The modernists' writing style is powerful enough to conceal the defects of their style, yet these defects are serious. In introducing characters, they often use the style of a dramatist. The modernists depict them at the outset of the story rather than letting them develop gradually. They also present them as types rather than as individuals through whose actions their type may be perceived. The modernists have written as critics exposing the ills of their respective societies.

In the history of modern Persian prose or writing style, Jamalzadeh is considered to be the one who started and introduced the technique. Another facet of his writing is his Dickensian flow of words with adjectives piled up, numerous repetitions and popular phrases never omitted where they can possibly be squeezed out. Jamalzadeh allows his copious literary memory to run freely when he takes pen in hand. However, the impression reflected from his literary techniques is that he never looks over a manuscript once he has completed it. Another serious defect is his negligence in revision and his careless disregard for form. This was a peculiar problem mainly for the modernist writers.

With regard to his writings, there appears to be a sharp distinction between the early stories written by Jamalzadeh and his later literary works. The prime themes of his early writings comprise conciseness, the novelty of form, originality of ideas and a biting sense of humour. His later works show a tendency towards prolixity, sage remarks and mystical and philosophical speculations, frequent use of classical poetry and, at times, lack of shape and order. Everyday expressions adorn almost every line, to the extent that his penchant for juxtaposing idioms seems to override other considerations.

With respect to Iranian society and literature, modernists' contributions come in the form of the content of their work and several issues they take up in their literary works. They are representatives of their times and the growing number of young intellectuals of Iran. One of the important thrusts of their writings is an analysis of the sociological problem of western foreign returned students in their own country. The contradictions of the native country are reflected in social prejudices and the predominance of selfish, influential classes with no sense of civil responsibilities, which were contested by young, idealistic and ambitious students.

Another theme with the modernists is criticism of Muslim clergy and Shiite rites and institutions in Iran. It is widely said that though brought in highly religious conditions compared to today's young generation, they present a critical view of the Muslim clergy and religious institutions. Unlike Sadique Hedayat, who abhorred everything about religious institutions and regarded them as evil, which was the outcome of the Arab conquest that suppressed the true Iranian ideals, Jamalzadeh's approach to religion was more sympathetic. He did not regard the religious establishment as necessarily evil but rather saw the clergy as only falling short of religious ideals and requirements.

The majority of modern Iranian writers do not know enough about the clerical mind and terminology and limit themselves to merely abusing the clergy. For instance, they abuse clergy by making bare statements like clergy are a vile collection of reactionary hypocrites who hinder progress. On the other hand, Jamalzadeh, with his religious background, is not a blind critic of the clergy. Rather, he beats the *akhund* with his own stick and defeats them. The 'Jahanam-i-ta'asub' stands as testimony to this aspect of Jamalzadeh. He does not abuse them but makes them actually appear in words and gestures as reactionary, ignorant, prejudiced, selfish and a blight of society.

The modernist trend mainly portrays social criticism. They are primarily concerned with middle class problems and shortcomings and blame the young middle class students for their naiveté. They show them victimised by charlatans of power and influence, thwarted by fear and seduced by vain fancies. They are concerned about the outmoded institution of marriage and the rights of women. They summed up the social ill of the country in their respective works as Jamalzadeh's "Namak-i-gandida" (Rotten salt) discusses the problems of corruption in the professional circles and thinking of the ordinary middle class in the following words that the bone of contention for any sort of corruption is very much relative to the destitution and hardship. So, this is as long as people are afraid of empty stomachs and the threat of oppression, they must bear with the corrupt morals in their attitude. So, circumstances are the most important factor in letting anyone be corrupt.

If someone has to understand the role of the modernist trend and their writing styles, he/she has to go through the constitutional revolution from 1905 to 1911. During these years, a new sort of writing style emerged in Iranian society, and it changed the course of Persian literature. While classical poetry had always been there in the form of panegyrics at the Qajar court, it was poetry which was mainly focused on political content and social and political satire that dominated the scene. But the fact can be denied that the old poetic forms such as the Malawi (a poem in couplets), ghazal, qasida, etc., were still used with the topical and political. The press played a more important role than anything to popularise prose and poetry.

Many modernist writers and poets who had depended for their living upon various patrons were no longer compelled to write panegyrics for the kings and the rulers. Even the common people started viewing their opinions by their writing skills. The prose and poetry had become the effective medium for satire and political discussion. The Iranians felt and lived with no boundations anymore while expressing their thoughts by their writing skills.

Most of the works of the time depict the role of political leaders in the Iranian revolution. However, very rarely has it been mentioned in the writings that literature has had a great influence and impact on the Iranian revolution. Though there has been enough evidence that clearly talks about the revolution of 1979 with its political purges and dramatic social upheavals, and the social problems shown have presented researchers with new themes and topics, at first, the most established Persian writers continued pursuing their original concerns, the struggle against the injustices of the former regime, the drive for freedom of thought and speech, and of the press. These aspirations coincided with the initial goals of the revolutionary movement. Persian short stories have been in new directions; new authors, with the help of the modernist trend, created works worthy of notice, made a social impact on the people and encouraged them to think differently for this literary revolution. The writer's biographical sketches have been drawn in the history of literature or encyclopedias, and their art of story writing has been discussed by scholars in Iran and abroad, but no single work exists that the modernistic approach has made a changed society and left an impact on the new era of Iran.

With this background, This book takes into account the contribution of these inventive writers' contribution to the world of Persian literature. Their critical comprehension of Iranian society is marked by their several writings and different forms of writing that were new to Persian literature. This books is an attempt to understand and elaborate several facets of innovations in the writings of their times that were characterised by uniqueness to their contemporary world.

Socio-political and Cultural Conditions of Iran in the 20th Century.
(Before Iranian Revolution 1979)

The Historical background of Reza Shah's reign: -

a) Brief Introduction of Iran and its History: -

Iran, once known as "Persia", is situated in the Central-West of Asia. It is one of the world's oldest continuing major civilisations and is one of the few states that are comprised, in particular, of humanity. It is situated in a highly important strategic position within the Middle East. During the 19th and 20th centuries, it was directly situated between the geographical spheres of British and Russian influences. It is said that Iran has never been colonised. However, it was very much influenced by the British and Russian governments in its internal politics. In 1907, the British and the Russians signed an agreement that divided Iran into three geographical spheres. Northern Iran was influenced by the Russian Empire, including Isfahan, Yazd, and the mountainous range of Zolfoqar. Southern Iran was under the influence of Britishers bordering Afghanistan, which was the sea of Oman, a little part of Yazd and Abbas port. The rest of the territories were declared as a neutral zone. The agreement came under fierce attack by the Iranian government. However, the British and the Russians had complete control over their specified zones. This agreement was in effect until 1915 when both Britain and Russia had a significant military presence in their specified area of influence[1].

Later on, in 1915, a new agreement was reached between Britain and Russia, according to which the neutral areas were to be further divided between the two powers. This was the time when Iran was influenced and

---

[1] Yahaiya Aryanpur, AzSaba-ta-Nima (2), Tehran 1372

divided between the British and the Russians. There was an agreement that the Russians would keep 11,000 Cossacks in the northern territories, and the British would keep 11,000 South Persian Rifles (southern police) in the south. After the October revolution, the newly established Bolshevik government officially cancelled all previous agreements, and the 1915 agreement practically collapsed. This led to the withdrawal of all Russian military presence from Iranian territory. Following the withdrawal of Russian forces from the northern territories, the British moved some of their constabulary from India to Baluchistan and sent their remaining military force to Hamadan, Qazvin, and Baku. This result somehow noted down that during the end of World War 1st entire, Iran came under the influence of the British Empire. This was one of the reasons that the presence of British troops in various parts of the country had greatly reduced Iranian sovereignty and independence. Iran started facing a lot of hurdles, including social disunity, tribal and ethnic conflict, political disorder, economic hardship and national poverty[2].

b) The Relations With the Russians and the British: -

On the other side Russian troops were withdrawn by the Bolshevik regime which consequently created a vacuum in the balance of power. The Iranian government anxiously tried to prevent the British from filling this vacuum. This led to marked hostility towards the British. During January 1918, with the denial of Tsarist privileges; a new wave of popular and official Anglophobia spread through Iran. There were growing demands from the British for a kindlier attitude on the part of Iran.

The British were very much calculative about their situation and wanted to safeguard their regional and local interests. Britain was very good with political and diplomatic supremacy, as highlighted by the Anglo-Persian Agreement of 1919. The Britishers always wanted to negotiate with their own policy, and then they went on to reach some local leaders and politicians in order to influence their ideas with the Iranians, whereby the Iranian government would employ British military, civil and technical advisers to reorganise the army and the state administration. This was the

---

2. YaqubAzand, Tarikh-i-AdabiyatNavin Iran, Tehran 1266

tactic of Britain. Through this, They wanted to have military, administrative and financial protectorate over Iran[3].

Internationally, the League of Nations did not acknowledge the 1919 agreement as binding and internally, the 1919 agreement aroused overwhelming protest from all sections of Iranian society[4].

Therefore, when the Soviet government sent an ultimatum demanding the evacuation of all British military forces from Iran in November 1920, it was received favourably by both the government and the public[5].

c) The Socio-political Impact During the Contemporary Period: -

During the month of October, Iranians rebelled and created an altogether new situation in the political arena of Iran as well as in general. This was one of the reasons that revolution started taking place and soon became an internal socio-political situation. The new Bolshevik government revoked all previous treaties that were damaging to Iran. However, the entry of the Bolshevik forces into the northern territories of Iran and the spread of communist ideology, together with internal instability, weak and ineffective central government, and the absence of a united national army, created a far more serious threat to the totality of Iranian territory than ever before. Furthermore, the conceivable collapse of northern Iran to the Bolsheviks made the threat of communism seem even more imminent[6].

In the beginning socio-political situation of Iran was uncertain and unstable to such an extent that the national unity of Iran was under threat. This was the time when Iran was practicing foreign policies and faced social relations were severely tensed, and the central government was weak and futile.

The inherent weakness of the government was reflected in the numerous cabinet reshuffles and continual changes in the government. Political instability had reached such a level that in the space of one year, six cabinets were formed, Prime Minister after Prime Minister came to power achieving

---

[3.] History of Iran, Constitutional Revolution 1906-1911, Iran Chamber Society, Tehran

مرتضی راوندی. جلداول،تاریخ اجتماعی ایران، 1353ق،تهران.

[5.] Bahar [Malekol So'ara] (1357 SH/1978).

[6.] Ibid.

very little while chaos and disorder continued. Political uncertainty was both affected by and, in turn, had an effect on social instability. Effectively, it was noticed that delicate and unpredictable social relations were further weakened as each group of social elites fought hard to maintain the status quo and safeguard their privileges.

d) The role of admiration of that time: -

The lack of a strong bonding and central administration had proved beneficial for various autonomous and semi-autonomous groups such as the 'clergy, tribal chieftains, major landlords, Qajar princes, the various revolutionaries, rebels and bandits.' An unstable government proved again and again the autonomy, power, and survival of these various groups. Regional self-autonomy, powerful tribal chieftains, financially independent and interfering 'clergy, and civil disintegration, in turn, further weakened the central government.' For example, the clergy dominated all judicial, educational and cultural affairs of the country.

In the words of court poet Mohammad Taqi Bahar (a key political figure at the time):

"The Shah was about to flee, political figures were preoccupied with power, position and obtaining a place in the cabinet, and rebels were killing, plundering and acquiring wealth. Journalists were involved in printing obscenities against their rival groups or promoting a particular political party at the expense of another. Competing political parties paid large sums to journalists to slander the opposition. Intellectuals had formed various political groups, set-up numerous papers, and were involved in internal fighting and backstabbing. The commercial classes were anxious and feared the loss of their property due to social, economic and political insecurity. The average national income had greatly decreased. Iran had become increasingly dependent on foreign loans, and her financial future seemed bleak and uncertain.[7]"

The political uncertainty of the country was further complicated by the social structure and the natural geography of Iran. This was the condition

---

[7] Bahar [Malekol So'ara] (1357 SH/1978), pp. 55-6. Yafiya DulatabadI and 'Abdollah Bahrain! both important political figures of the time give a similar account as that of Bahar.

when the entire Iran was set on isolation. This was the time when Iran had not built up a strong economic power and it had to suffer a lot due to this[8].

The combination of the factors stated above had loosened the very cement which held the social mosaic together. It is often argued that Shi'ism played an important role in the national unity of Iran. If one accepts this assumption, the role of the clergy becomes even more significant and substantial. During that period, people who mainly belonged to part of the revolution or largely participated in protests were from the villages, and they were badly misguided or manipulated by the so-called upper-class who thought they were leading the movement. They were mainly the elite class and had control over politics.

The local leaders and clergy class were the mediator between these two groups. The Iranian population was entirely at the mercy of this small group of society. The so-called elite groups were often involved in conserving and maintaining their own territory of influence, even at the cost of endangering the national unity of Iran. The elite class, considered to be one of the active ones, was generally tied up with the imperialist power to maintain their supremacy through internal instability. Foreign military intervention and political disintegration had exacerbated the prevailing regional disorder to such an extent that the strength and autonomous tendencies of local powers vis-à-vis the central government took on an unparalleled magnitude.

The peasantry was the largest class instrumental in the richness of the Iranian culture and civilisation. The tribal constituted 15 percent of the total population of Iran in 1920 and remained completely untouched by modern advances of any kind. The level of literacy was negligible among these two communities. Tribal and peasantry classes were mostly marginalised. They were mainly guided by their local leaders or landlords who generally used to rule them[9].

The dominance of the elites was so comprehensive that peasantry and tribal classes would not even be able to decide about their own personal life. They were largely guided by the clergy class. Women, who made up half of the population of Iran, were deprived of any role other than motherhood.

---

8. Zabih, S., *The Communist Movement in Iran,* Berkeley: University of CaliforniaPress, 1966
9. Ibid

Even that particular role was limited, as they did not have any legal rights in relation to their children. Women were deprived of any social or political involvement. They did not have the right to vote or to employment and had limited access to public places.

It was the time of the First World War, and the effects lasted until 1921. Due to this war, trouble cabinets, which were mainly formed by its so-called anarchy government, ended with no conclusion. The political situation was in a condition to think further and establish their own set-up of governance. The exercise of governmental authority came to a virtual standstill. The consulates of Britain and Russia, as well as the British-owned telegraph offices, became the real seats of power in the provinces.

Political refugees often used these offices as places of sanctuary in much the same way as they would use a religious shrine. Russian, British and Turkish troops occupied various parts of the country. Wassmuss, a German agent, was active in southern Iran, organising tribal resistance to Britain. To substitute the Swedish-led Iranian gendarmerie and to counterbalance the Russian-commanded Persian Cossack Brigade, the British organised the South Persia Rifles. Brigandage, tribal lawlessness and highway robbery were alarming. In fact, highwaymen, in the absence of authority, often raided towns and sometimes remained, wrecking all economic activity. These were the political happenings, and due to this, Reza Khan came into power. Many historians often argue that the original engineer of the coup was a young journalist named Syed Mohammad Hussain Tabataba'I. On the morning of 26 February 1921, when the people of Tehran woke up, they found the streets plastered with posters. They read 'I command!' and were all signed by Reza, Commander-in-Chief of all the Armed Forces[10].

Syed Ziya'o din became premier, but there was little doubt about where the real power used to play. It was against such a background that Reza Khan emerged as a dominant political figure. After the 1921 coup of Syed Ziya'o din and the Cossacks, Reza Khan soon rose through the ranks of the army and entered the political scene. His first post was as commander. He went on to become Minister of War and then Commander-in-Chief of the Armed Forces. In 1923 he became Prime Minster, and finally, in 1925, he

---

10. Wilber, D. N., *Riza Shah Pahlavi: The Resurrection and Reconstruction of Iran, 1878-1944,* New York: Exposition, 1975.

was crowned as the King of kings. Somehow, it was very much clear that the coup had been intended by the British as an alternative route to the achievement of the 1919 Agreement, namely the political stabilisation of Iran, which would not pose a threat to the main local and regional interests of the British Empire[11].

e) The Reza Shah's Ideas of his nation: -

Reza Shah was known for his autocratic rule. He was considered to be a dictatorship established through terror and the brutal destruction of all those who stood in his way. The other most commonly agreed point is that Reza Shas's rule put an end to 'provincial kingdoms', regionalism, sectarianism, tribal fiefdoms, etc. He was the one who can be blamed for civil wars and local movements against the government in Iran. Reza Shah thought of modernising the country by putting in its collective effort, but somewhere, he was badly criticised for not seeking the help and advice of his own people. This may be one of the reasons that the people of Iran boycotted and set on to build the idea called revolution. This was also the nature of Reza Shah's rule, which betrayed many morals and goals of the constitutional revolution, such as civil liberties and parliamentary rule[12].

All through his reign, Reza Shas introduced and finished numerous extraordinary arrangements in Iran, which were achieved at the cost of sacrificing the goals and aspirations of the constitutional revolution. He was the one who tried to change the root of Iranian society. However, despite the many new institutional developments, social relations remained exceptionally very much the same, though the changes also affected its economy and put Iran on its back foot. The education system was badly ruined, and the debate among Iranian scholars took place that Shah's policy to achieve something at the cost of Iranian heritage was not suitable at all and must be condemned. This was not justified by the scholars and the progressive people of the society. It was also discussed that building up modern Iran may require some changes, but those changes cannot be its heritage[13].

[11.] Jacqz, J. (ed.), Iran: Past, Present and Future, New York: Aspen Institute forHumanistic Studies, 1976.

[12.] Lenczowski, G. (ed.), Iran under the Pahlavis, Stanford, California: HooverInstitution Press,1978.

[13.] Ibid

f) An analytical understanding of Pahlavi's reign.

The regime of Reza Shah was mostly viewed or observed as a drastic change in Iranian history. The European influence was at its peak, whether in language or culture. It was the time when westernisation was badly injected into the Iranian culture. Iranians were badly affected by "that disease", as recounted by some of the local and traditional leaders of Iran. The westernisation was forced upon the people. The idea behind penetrating this culture was to let this Iranian culture be opened to the West. At that time, Iran was or is considered a Muslim country, and it was thought that westernisation was just the opposite of Islam. So, the Islamists boycotted this cultural revolution. Since changes were introduced all of a sudden, it led to a massive reaction in the form of an assertion of national identity. It has also been seen that the process of changing the old Iran to the new Iran was very much simultaneous because Reza Shah always wanted to have command over the country and its people, meaning thereby he proposed to be an Anarchist and never wanted to let his reign fall down. He did not appreciate even a single circumstance which was against him, and he never thought of inviting their own country's people to sit and discuss the future of Iran. This may be one of the reasons that he was often criticised by the progressive sections of the society. He was also called or quoted by the people that the Shah of this country was being controlled by outsiders, mainly western powers. It can also be argued that the supporters were very much in favour of their king, and they mainly benefitted from him. Reza Shah did not choose to decide the destiny of his country; instead, he quoted the word that he believed in modernisation from conservatism.

Reza Shah always knew that the society of Iran could be controlled by the administrative forces. So, he planned to control the administration along with military dominance. The same situation took place during the Qajar dynasty as well. The conspiracy was also set-up for a long time ago in Iran to break the unity among the Iranians. However, the Reza Shah's regime marked a highly differentiated political and social structure. This was the time when Iran was suffering from a transitional phase with social instability, economic trouble and political unrest. Reza Shah thought that he was very constructive in making Iran's future in his own way by modernising it.

This process was attained by strengthening national unification and by establishing modern armed forces. During Reza Shah's regime, it was noticed that the people of Iran struggled a lot to maintain harmony in their country and fought to get basic rights. This was also the time when Iranian society was coming under the influence of the Shah's manipulators. Iranian society was politically damaged or culturally targeted. This was an open threat to their legacy, though.

Although significant changes were made by Reza Shah in his regime to the political institutions and some of the economic institutions, they were never considered as a development for the nation. The major part of the political system is headed by his own official under his confidence. The reason behind the strong Pahlavi regime was that it was supported by the strong military and bureaucracy, which consisted of the elite class and upper-class sections of the society. Reza Shah struggled to modernise the country's industrial infrastructure and culture, but his reforms did not fully extend to the political realm, and the basic political structure remained intact. The primary pillars of the Pahlavi dynasty were its military and its Bureaucrats, who managed to control the whole of Iran. This was the major difference between the Qajar and Pahlavi dynasties. During the Qajar rule, the main power was observed mostly by the Olama and Clergy class, but in Pahlavi, it came to the elite class, which was supposed to be modern or influenced by western society.

Reza Shah's efforts were influenced by the European "modernism." In Iran when it was introduced it was perceived to be a long period of far-reaching, profound and consequential changes and was not limited to the measures implemented or even envisaged during the 1960s and 1970s.

This was the period in which I noticed that the power of Olama had been limited and decentralised in a way to make Iran better in the present and in future. It may have withdrawn the Allies invasion and occupation of the country in 1941-1942. The foundations of the present government seem to have the structure followed by the Reza Shah's regime[14].

[14.] Casanova, Halpem (1963) & Black (1966) refer to the necessity of changing one's psychological system and Smith (1970) refers to this process as polity-transvaluational secularization.

The three main features of Iran's political history were generally considered- monocracy, external intervention and insurgency. These were the things which marked almost all stages of the Pahlavi regime. During Reza Shah's regime, it was clearly shown that revolutionary powers would not be exercised anymore. However, there were some other forces to challenge the power of that government.

Radical situations did not arise because the regime initially courted the support of those groups who could form potential blocks of opposition and then thought of finishing them. Meanwhile, the absence of disobedience to the administration, outside intercession and political absolutism were vital to the government. To a great extent, the authoritarian and self-assertive nature of political power under the Qajars was supplanted by a more precise standardisation of political power under the Pahlavi dynasty[15].

Efforts were made to assemble political power and expertise into the Pahlavi framework instead of emanating from individual political figures.

The Shah always believed that it was central to the survival of the system he had established. Foreign interference in the country's internal affairs also persisted during the Pahlavi era. Reza Shah assumed that only his direct personal control over the political process would save the country from chaos and from lapsing into socialism. He perceived this form of utilitarianism as necessary not only to maintain a strong personal hold of power but also in the effective hassle of central government's buff over the entire society.

Reza Shah had always been wanted to legitimise his regime by storing the memory and the quality of Iran's pre-Islamic past. But somehow, he failed to manage his legitimacy and could not maintain authenticity or to offer belief to his claim of awesome majesty. Reza Shah made an attempt to rule with reference to the pre-Islamic model of Persian kingship in an effort to adopt total power. He realised that if his reign were to be superimposed upon society, the socio-political culture of Iran would be changed.

It was anticipated that this would bring about a shift in public attitudes towards the form of authority of the ruler and concepts of rightfulness. It

---

15. Ibid.

was also assumed that during the reign of Reza Shah, these changes may have brought about a complete sacred-temporal dual power structure.

g) The social changes and adjustments during Reza Shah: -

This social adjustment would be achieved by releasing such matters as the law and its implementation, education from religious regulation, and expanding the jurisdiction of the state over these spheres. The questions of legitimate authority, who possesses it and who has the right to exercise it are pivotal for Islam. These concepts have played a crucial role in shaping not only the religious but also the political history of Iran. The whole idea was somewhere derived from the idea of Islam and its Imams. Reza Shah wanted to reduce the influence of religious values and institutions in the political and cultural spheres. It means that he had some sort of secular agenda. Reza Shah failed to do so because, in Iran, religious beliefs were widespread not only among the Olamas but also among the larger public. Due to the dual power structure of politics and hierocracy, political loyalty could easily shift to one of the 'Olama if the ruler did not have religious legitimacy.' The polarisation of Iranian society had nurtured different attitudes towards the forms of authority[16].

Reza Shah always thought the separation of religion and political power. This, up to some extent, was completed during his reign but the internal structure of Iranian society was far slower to change, and the impact of Olama over Iranian masses stayed almost intact.

The Shah wished to restrict the self-governing system of religious institutions and tried to influence it by subordinating it to secular power. However, this policy was part of a greater policy of reducing all other alternative sources of power and was not specifically directed at the Olama.

---

[16] Casanova suggests that four related and simultaneously unfolding developments - the Protestant Reformation, the rise of the modern state, the rise of modern capitalism, and the rise of modern science set in motion the dynamics of the process which undermined the medieval religious system of classification. Each of the four developments contributed its own dynamic to modern processes of secularization and was one of the carriers of the process of modernization. If one accepts this assumption, it follows that one should expect different historical patterns of secularization. As each of these carriers developed different dynamics in different places at different times, the pattern and the outcome pf historical processes should vary accordingly. Only when it comes to capitalism has it been nearly universally recognized that there is a positive correlation between rates of secularization and rates of economic development, urbanization, industrialization, proletarianization, and education.

Reza Shah sought to implement the power of the central government by establishing a professional standing army, a uniform judiciary, the rule of law, and uniform secular education, and by curbing the power of 'Olama' integrating rural Iran, major landowners and all other alternative sources of power into the central government. These bourgeois reforms did not fundamentally change the fabric of Iranian society or the structure of social relations. Throughout this period, as the power of the central government increased, so the political power and influence of the Olama decreased. Overall, Reza Shah wanted to crack the monopoly of these Olamas, and he, up to some level, succeeded[17].

h) Understanding the theory of Modernism throughout the period.

The theory developed by Reza Shah was the total transformation of the Iranian economy into a semi-industrialised and commercialised system. The extension of the power of the central government over all sections of society with the purpose of centralisation and unification would help in achieving this particular goal. In the process of achieving these two basic attempts, the government attempted to eliminate traditional social forces and ideologies and substitute them with ideologies and attitudes seen to be more compatible with its 'modem' aims. In this way, it had a significant effect on religion and religious foundations. Reza Shah's first and most critical undertaking was to develop an army and disarm potential separatists, particularly migrant clans. Later, he found a way to curb the power of the Olama and spread an official belief system of patriotism, drawing upon Iran's pre-Islamic past and criticising Arabs and the advice from Islam. His rule may be depicted as 'autocratic secular nationalism,' The social, financial and political changes in this period were unparalleled in Iranian history.

During the Reza Shah period, there was an expansion of central government intervention in the monetary sphere, which created new social groups. Their political orientation and economic viewpoints were in sharp contrast to the traditional middle class. A new social elite was formed around the government and the throne, whose main aim was to gain recognition and power to create a 'modern' society. The term' modem' is

---

[17]. Ibid.

regularly utilised to belong to the standard view of history, which considers industrialist innovation as an unavoidable result or even natural law. Modernity occurs during the evolutionary process leading from early forms of exchange and social structure forced by the 'irrational forces' of tradition to the economic and social rationality of the middle class.

This specific comprehension of modernity belongs to a view of history that cuts across the great divide between industrialist and non-industrialised societies. It treats industrial laws of motion as if they were the universal laws of history. It is important to point out that even anti-modernism can have a similar effect on naturalising capitalism, as can be seen in the sociological speculations. It has been seen that modern history has a long process of rationalisation. The rationalisation of the state in governmental organisation and the rationalisation of the economy in industrial capitalism were two major aspects of modernisation in Europe. The impact of this procedure, the progress of reason and freedom most often associated with the Enlightenment, has been to allow humanity from traditional restraints. But at the same time, rationalisation produces and disguises new oppression; this view of history makes capitalism inevitable and, at the very least, naturalises it. Equating capitalism with modernity disguises the specificity of not only capitalism but modernity as well. It is commonly agreed that the reform policies of Reza Shah 'modernised' and fundamentally changed the living style of Iranian society. However, the extent to which the formation of the Pahlavi State can be viewed in terms of a continuity of a set of historical processes or a state with complete law and order by Reza Shah[18].

i) The Various Approaches to the Reza Shah Regime: -

With respect to the above descriptions, two sets of arguments are generally made. The primary perspective is the emergence of the political system between the second half of the nineteenth-century and the first half of the twentieth in terms of an important change that resulted in a significant break from the past[19].

---

[18]. Zirinsky, M. P, 'Imperial Power and Dictatorship: Britain and theRise of Reza Shah,' *IJMES*
[19]. Browne, E. G, *A History of Persian Literature in Modern Times*, Cambridge

The Reza Shah period is seen as the start of the process of transformation of Iran from pre-capitalism to capitalism, where the focus was to decentralise the power and modernise its centres. The second model of argument sees the stated period in terms of an underlying historical continuity. Within this perspective, the Pahlavi regime is viewed as a neo-patrimonial state, a historical continuation of the patrimonial (Asiatic despotism) rule of the Qajars. Most of the research agreed that Reza Shah's period has been affected by one of these hypothetical models. The Reza Shah period has been considered either in terms of a historical continuity of patrimonial or Asiatic authoritarianism, re-emerging under modem conditions as neo-patrimonialism[20].

There have been some theoretical problems with both representations. The social essentialists display and propose that the events of the past determine and limit the possibilities of future development. One winning argument as far as the Middle East is that the Islamic' substance' is responsible for the shortcomings or formative 'disappointment' of the region. Despotism is viewed as the very idea of Islam and political conduct restricted by crippling Islamic social structures. The Islamic legacy is seen as a hindrance to all consequent advancement. Additionally, this theory frustrates to take global and peripheral forces into account.

As far as it matters, the main model neglects to represent the specificity of Iranian political and social procedures. The basic constraints of the hypothesis disregard the particular qualities of the Iranian case. The later structural account sees Iran in terms of the dependence of the 'peripheral' state on the world order that maintains it as an agent. It is 'external' to the social relations and institutions over which it governs. Iran's condition seems to be always in a dilemma due to the nature of that country, either Islamic or Secular[21].

Based on the first perception, it is argued that there is a profound discontinuity between Iran and the First World. Reza Shah's rule was essentially different from that of previous monarchies in Iran. Under Reza

---

[20] Ibid.

[21] For a detailed account of the various changes that were introduced during this period please refer to thesection entitled Reforms of Reza Sah, pp. 321-328.

Shah, the state controlled the whole of the national territory, whereas the Qajar did not extend and control the rest of their territories.

The Reza Shah's government intervened, controlled and promoted economic development, whereas the other government abandoned it. This was happening for the first time in Iran's history, when a large modern standing army, a centralised secular legal system, and secular mass state education were being supported.

These institutional changes were extraordinary, as were the cultural and social reforms introduced, such as the uniform dress code and compulsory unveiling. The Pahlavi government was constituted on a completely new basis - that of military dictatorship. Reza Shah's rule provided some of the necessary pre-conditions for the conversion of Iran to capitalism. Within this model of argument, there is no substantive continuity between the Pahlavi regime and the regimes of previous centuries. There were some very big differences between the two governments. Comparatively, the Reza Shah regime has been somewhat appreciated by the upper section of society but strictly criticised by the rural Iranians[22].

This set of arguments has been viewed as a systematic process of historical development; the evolution from pre-capitalism to capitalism is supposedly an inside to a worldwide setting. The specificity of Iranian inner procedures is put inside a worldwide setting. Dependency theory includes an extensive collection of writing that fuses numerous ideas and strategies; however, the recognising highlight of all dependency theory is that the social and economic development of 'underdeveloped' countries is viewed as conditioned by external forces. Within this perspective, Middle Eastern states are forms of the peripheral state, shaped by relations of dependency on the major capitalist powers of the centre. Dependency both anticipates bona fide financial improvement and undermines the authenticity of the modernising state in that it neglects to convey what it guarantees. The externalisation of the state from society in the Islamic world is not the historical outcome of 'Asiatic despotism' but instead the significant making of the capitalist world market. The state, by reason of its dependence on the

---

[22] Roxborough, I., *Theories of Underdevelopment*, London: Macmillan, 1979.

world market, arranges the social development that is administered as per the requirements of the world market.

It has been for sure that it not only governs common society but also nullifies it by accepting every one of its capacities. The economy, group, religion, instruction and family are altogether infiltrated by the state. It derives its power mainly from its dependence on central powers rather than an internal power base. The state is financially arranged to separate surplus esteem; ideologically, this was happening for the first time in Iranian history under the banner of development and modernisation, whereby people are compulsorily modernised[23].

In developing nations, the financial part of the state is particularly articulated since the shortcoming of the indigenous middle class has tended to draw the state even more into a monetarily official position than has been the situation in the more created industrialist nations. This articulated role of the state under the conditions of capitalist development has been especially recognisable in Iran. The argument of the state and class interests represented, therefore, becomes essential to the analysis of the economic transformation in Iran[24].

The Iranian state was not, as in many other Asian and African countries, a post-colonial state in the sense of owing its very existence to the link between local officials and imperial states outside. Rather, the Iranian state was created in a relatively independent way[25].

It must be brought up that the connection amongst state and society has been presently advancement in the course of the most recent century and this development has brought about various diverse conjunctures at various crossroads in Iranian history. It is only by ignoring this history that it becomes possible to present the problem as a confrontation between the community and the state without considering the essential socio-political advancements of a national kind[26].

---

[23] Ibid.

[24] Ibid.

[25] It must be pointed out that the historical links between the British and Reza Shah's consolidation of power are well documented. Furthermore, the power play between Britain and Russia also had great significance for government formation in Iran.

[26] Halliday, F, Iran Dictatorship and Development, London: Harmondsworth, Penguin, 1978. pp. 21-36

The secondary argument has been viewed as the stated period in terms of a fundamental historical continuity. Within this view, the Pahlavi regime is viewed as a neo-patrimonial state, a historical continuation of the patrimonial (Asiatic despotism) rule of the Qajars. In other words, it is argued that there is a historical and systematic continuation, as Iran is an Asiatic country where despotism is an inevitable feature of political life. Patrimonial forces continued and were still influential even under the modernising attempts of Reza Shah. This argument operates within the theoretical framework of 'social essentialism', which views obstacles to development as overwhelmingly internal and unchanging during the last 1400 years of Islamic history. The rationale of this presumption is that the present in any given history contains the greater part of that history in its structure.

This is the fundamental precept of social essentialism. Its supporters have tried to clarify the Reza Shah period in terms of the continuity of persevering patrimonial impacts in the political field. Imported European modernisation at the levels of both foundation and ideation brought about the development of a neo-patrimonial state instead of a modem nation-state. Meaning that it helps to make a distinction between social specificity and cultural essentialism. Social specificity is contended regarding specific inborn and constantly dynamic social components which support certain socio-political advancements and restrain others.

In Iran's history or in Islamic countries' imported' European modernisation resulted not in the formation of the nation-state but rather in 'neo-patrimonial states,' The failure of the modem nation-state in the Islamic world is due to the following factors: failure of the 'law-state' and consequently failure of democracy, nation formation, continuation of regionalism and separateness of border from the centre.

Within this perspective, each historical period in a particular country is the manifestation of that particular cultural essence. This theory fails to take global and external forces into account. Cultural essentialist theories view secularisation as the key component of the development of capitalism and democracy in the West and the unsuccessful development of both in other societies. Modernisation is seen as synonymous with capitalist development and secularisation.

Moreover, in terms of Islamic societies, its expectations are based on the widely-held misconception present among Muslims and non-Muslims that Islam is both a religion and a state, an inherent theocracy, which, when examined closely, does not hold to be historically accurate. Although there is no institutionalised priesthood in Islam, overall, the clergy class played a crucial and decisive role in the political realm. This informally structured institution acted in a formalised and collective manner. People who followed Islam have certainly played a formative role in shaping Iranian culture; Iran's pre-Islamic culture, however, is also of equal importance. The language, mythology, and historic identity of Iran have, to some extent, preserved their pre-Islamic past. The interplay of these two forces - Shi'i Islam and the pre-Islamic heritage has made Iran's reaction to the West extremely complex and also different from the rest of the Middle East. This is why secularisation and modernism have been the main course undertaken by Reza Shah Pahlavi. In his sixteen years of rule, he made some important changes in the context of Iran's development. These were mainly the roads, the Trans-Iranian Railway was built, modern education was introduced, the University of Tehran was established, and for the first time, systematic dispatch of Iranian students to Europe was started. The country's industrialisation stepped up, and its achievements were great.

A Critical Study of Modernistic Trends in Iran

a) The Beginning of the Idea of Modernist Trends: -

This chapter discusses how these modernist trends focus on revolutionary fiction, including the short story, which is marked by dynamic experimentation with techniques of narration, choice of plot, imagery, and structure. It also deals with the analytical study of Persian Literature in Iran. In line with recent tendencies in most modern literature, modern Persian fiction expresses doubts, uncertainty, anxiety, tension, paradox, and dilemmas; it tells of beginnings and not of ends. It deals with realism as a case in point of literature.

Iran has always been a conspicuous case to discuss and bring into the academic discourse in central Asia. If someone has to understand Iran's history as well as its literary contribution, especially from 1906 to 1979, the contextual socio-political set-up of Iran becomes fundamental to understanding. At the time when Iran was at its peak of revolution, Reza Shah Pahlavi was boycotted by their own people, and it was widely debated whether Iran should remain a monarchy or become either an Islamic republic or a democracy[27].

This was the period which determined the development and progression of Iran as a nation-state. Before the revolution, the predominant clergy class enjoyed a lot of authority. Changes brought during this period unleashed a series of forces that transformed and reshaped the face of Iranian society in every aspect imaginable way. These changes have rocked not only the political and economic spheres of Iran but, even more fundamentally, culture and society. These changes have negatively affected people's social, political and economic status in Iran. Indeed, the clerical revolutionaries at the outset of the revolution suggested that their goals were not aimed at

---

[27] Yahiya Aryanpur, Az Saba-ta-Nima (2),Tehran 1372.

economic transformation but rather the maintenance and continuation of the law of God, as interpreted by the clerics. With the Islamists in power, the new clerical elite came back to an earlier time in the seventh-century, where, in their view, society in Arabia was at its zenith under the rule of the Koran. Consequently, the Islamic fundamentalists became the "architects" to inject the same Islamic fundamentalist values and norms into modern twentieth-century Iran[28]. None of the policies implemented by the Islamic government after the revolution has been as backwards-looking and misguided at both the personal and a broader societal and cultural level than what has been the regime's stance on issues concerning their people. The social and political emancipation of people was only one reason behind the clerical revolt against the monarchy. The Shahs made a conscious and systematic effort to exclude clerical control of Iranian society[29]. For example, the clergy were excluded from their traditional spheres of control in such areas as the judiciary and education. The Islamic revolution, at its core, was nothing more than a reactionary attempt by a threatened class (namely the clergy) fearing a loss of material, legal, and moral influence, successfully reasserting itself in order to prevent the transfer of power to a newly created modern bureaucratic state system. If one examines this paradigm and applies it to the eighteen years since the Islamists came to power, one can see that the policies were adopted and implemented not so much on the basis of ideology but rather for the purpose of continuation and survival of the existing Islamic fundamentalist state[30]. Therefore, the idea of making Iran an Islamic Republic of Iran was also boycotted by some of the people who thought of implementing full-fledged democracy rather than imposing Islam or Islamic State on Iran, and since then, there have been many agitations by different societal and economic elements within society, proposing reforms in the Islamic republic.

b) The role of Naser o-Din Shah and Mozafar o-Din Shah: -

During the 1900s, the best way to spare the nation from government defilement and outside control was to make a composed code of laws. This

---

[28] Iran: State of Terror, Parliamentary Human Rights Group (1996).

[29] Ibid.

[30] ALATTOTF. KAMRANT, the Politics of Writing in Iran: A History of Modern Persian Literature, (Syracuse University Press, 2000). Pp. 264.

sentiment caused the constitutional revolution. There had been a series of ongoing covert and overt activities against Naser o-Din Shah's despotic rule, for which many had lost their lives. The effort of flexibility contenders at long last proved to be fruitful amid the rule of Mozafar o-Din Shah. Mozafar o-Din Shah rose to the position of power in June 1896. In the wake of the determined endeavours of flexibility contenders, Mozafar o-Din Shah of Qajar Line was compelled to issue the declaration of the constitution and the making of a chosen parliament (the Majlis) on August 5, 1906. The imperial power was constrained, and a parliamentary framework was built.

The economic growth was good at its best during that time. However, the opposition against Reza Shah was at large because of his policy to give Savak control of the country. The opposition was mainly led by Khomeini, who was exiled to Iraq and later on to France. In January 1979, Shah left Iran and handed the country's command to Shapour Bakhtiar, who failed to manage the worst situation in that country, and finally, civil war took place. During the month of April 1979, a national referendum took place, and Ayatollah Khomeini declared an Islamic republic with a new constitution reflecting his ideals of Islamic government[31].

"Shah Raft" ("The Shah Went"): Mohammad Reza Shah and his family leave Iran on January 15, 1979 amidst growing popular demonstrations against the monarchy. *Ettela'at newspaper, January 16, 1979*

Protesters around **Shahyad Tower** *(later Azadi Tower),* **Tehran,** *1979.(Courtesy: Reuters)*

c) A Glimpse of Modern Persian Literature: -

The literature (Modern Persian literature) or the literary activities and Socio-political Transformations pertain to the writings from the twentieth-

---

[31.] 5. History of Iran, Constitutional Revolution 1906-1911, Iran Chamber Society.

century. As that century drew to a close and the present one commenced, critics began to show a lively interest in the literature of that period. Major new studies from markedly different points of view have been published. Kamran Talattof has proposed a new and innovative approach to the understanding of Modern Persian literature. This he calls "episodic literary movement,"[32] a theory that brings political and social conditions into sharp focus. Briefly, he argues that political and social conditions at any given time produce a pertinent "ideology of representation and that this ideology helps to shape, and is shaped by, a cluster of aesthetically significant literary texts" that constitute a "literary episode." Ideology is related to literature through a shared set of metaphors. The history of Persian literature is conventionally viewed as an integrated continuum. Because of the impact of ideology on the production of literature, the author defines the literary history of the modern period as a "series of distinct episodes distinguishable by their ideology of representation. Thus, the literary history of this period moves by 'episodes,' and these constitute, in effect, a new form of periodisation."

As far as the social content per se is concerned, there are almost six major themes. Some of them are particularly pertinent to this analysis of the social impact of the modernist literary trend: (1) opposition to the Pahlavi government, (2) rejection of aspects of Shii institutions and practices, (3) concern with alleged economic and social backwardness in Iran, (4) criticism of sterilisation, (5) expression of a sense of culture-specific alienation or loss of Iranian roots, and (6) Communication of a strong sense of cultural nationalism[33].

In the beginning, Persian prose writing used to be a medium for dispensing historical, philosophical and scientific knowledge, sometimes in the guise of autobiographies. Novels and short stories were rarely used, and emotional expressions were found chiefly in poetry. During the sixteenth to eighteenth century, the Persian prose style was both obscure and flowery in nature, and it reflected the formalised society of which the writers were a part. At the beginning of the nineteenth-century, increased cultural contact with Europe and social mobility created a desire for prose. This was strengthened by political movements, which later culminated

---

[32] Ibid.
[33] Iranian Studies (1968 - 1985).

in the Constitution of 1906[34]. However, the forerunners of modern prose writers recognised the clumsiness of the existing prose forms. Thus, their first effort was a stylistic reform, which sought to introduce a simple way of expression. The factors which contributed to this movement were:

- Travel books about Europe were written by kings, princes, businessmen, and scholars.

- Newspapers and journals.

- Translations of works of such European writers as Moliere and Dumas[35].

d) The literary renaissance: -

These literary events were responsible for the further development of prose along three lines: conservative realism, social realism, and social individualism. The conservative realism has resulted from the ideological influence of the Western Europe. Social realism was inspired by modern Soviet thinking, and finally, social individualism was a product of the rich Persian classics and humanistic values. A good representative of conservative realism is Mohammad Hijazi, who wrote his first novel Homa in 1929, later Parichir in 1930, Andishe in 1940, and Ayene ("Mirror") in 1954.

Another writer of this group of conservative realists is Jamalzadeh, who founded short story writing in modern Iran. His first book, Yaki Bud, Yaki Nabud ("Once There Was, Once There Was Not", also known as Once-Upon-a-Time), was written and published in Berlin in 1921 and is a collection of six short stories. The first one, titled "Persian Is Sweet," presents the conflict between western-educated individuals who use foreign words in their everyday spoken language, the clergy who use Arabic, and the ordinary Persian who is lost between the two. It finally concludes that the sweetness of the Persian language has some claim on both the traditional Arabic-oriented speech of the clergy and the modernist tendency to employ foreign words[36]. Ali Dashti belongs to the same literary school. More than any other modern writer, he desires to give a picture of modern Persian

---

34. History of Iran, Constitutional Revolution 1906-1911, Iran Chamber Society.
35. Ibid.
36. Kamshad. H, Modern Persian Prose Literature, Pp 122.

women. He selects his characters from the upper-class, usually Western-oriented, wealthy, and attractive people. His women are frequently the product of two cultures, and he presents them as creatures wanting social equality without accepting social responsibility.

A writer who can be thought of as a link between conservative and social realism is the well-known critic Sa'aid Nafisi[37]. He is one of the first contributors to the modern prose in Iran and has translated quite a number of French writings. He is equally at home in almost all literary media: press, short stories, historical and social novels.

A representative of the literary school of social realism is Bozorg' Alavi, who wrote his first work in 1934. Influenced by Freud, he tries to interpret his characters in terms of Freudian psychology. Jalal-Al Ahmad is another writer from the social realist school. He takes his characters from the devoutly religious lower class and describes them sympathetically so as to reveal their mode of thinking. Sadiq Chubak is another social writer whose book 'Khayme Shab Bazi' contains eleven sections, each one being a real picture of daily life. Undoubtedly, the cultural contact of the Iranian elites with both Western Europe and Russia has contributed somewhat to these writings. A good representative of this group is Sadiq Hidayat, who is, perhaps, the greatest short story writer of modern Persian literature. His list of writings begins with "Zindeh-Bigur" ("Half Dead") in 1902, followed by many others, including "Sag-e-Virlgard" ("Street Dog") and "Buf-e-Kur" ("The Blind Owl"). The philosophies of humanism and nationalism inspired him to investigate and describe various social groups. His kind heart drew his attention to the life of the lower class, although he did not ignore other groups. He selected his characters and subjects with mastery and revealed their mode of life and mindset with great perceptive depth. This thorough understanding of the minds and emotions of people, plus his own deep sensitivity, gave him good reason to write. His works show both vertical and horizontal dimensions. He takes his readers to near and distant places at various times and introduces them to many groups of people who make up the world. He does not always write of the present but takes one to the wonders of the past, describes the adventures of early man and

---

[37] YaqubAzand, Tarikh-i-Adabiyat Navin Iran, Tehran 1266.

shows rationality above all. In the same vein, Dehkoda, a writer in the early twentieth-century, was a skillful satirist, as was Sadiq Hedayat.

This brief analysis discloses that the progress of modern Persian prose has been more a result of political writing than of pure literary activity[38]. Political unrest and a new evaluation of the place of man in society brought about special newspapers whose chief purpose was to awaken the people. It was necessary for writers to employ a simple style and direct their ideas toward public and national problems. Historians, translators and literary men were all involved in this movement. Inspiration came from European countries and Persian culture itself. As a result, three literary movements emerged, as we have seen.

e) The idea of creative writing in the context of Iranian society

For over a thousand years, creative Persian writing has more specifically and extensively than any other art medium reflected and sustained, particularly Iranian social subjects and introductions and has more than some other single indigenous phenomenon characterised Iranian culture for educated Iranians themselves, who during that time have regularly indicated this writing as an indication of their special place in and distinctive contributions to human social expression.

Presently, the expression "innovative Persian writing" refers to different customs in Iranian literature. There is a society custom that developed upon the foot sole areas of the presence of the neo-Persian dialect in the ninth century. At that point, a better-known custom was developed that started in a similar period that perseveres today, but without the custom of Iranian support, particularly verse, of artistic traditionalists who feel that the standards, structures, and subjects of artists from Rudaki (d. 940) to Jami (d. 1492) constitute still important prescriptive benchmarks. A third convention is that of Islamic devotional and Sufistic writing that developed inside and in response to Iran's customs and appeared to thrive amid such times of specific hardship as the outcome of the mid-thirteenth-century Mongol intrusions. Mongol intrusions have a different set of marks in Iranian literature compared to the modernistic trend.

---

[38] RYPKA, JAN, History of Iranian Literature, D. Reided Publishing Company Dordrecht- Holland 1068.

Finally, there is a modernist trend in Persian literature that began to develop in the early years of the 20th century, in part as a vehicle for the expression of then-nascent Iranian political nationalism. Owing much to 19th-and 20th-century western literature and constituting a revolutionary development vis-à-vis traditional literature both in its use of diction and style close to the language of everyday speech and in the representation of unprecedented subjects and themes mirroring individual views and concrete contemporary concerns, this modernist literature has been the dominant strain of Persian literature since World War II.

Finally, the modernist trend in Persian writing started to be created in the early years of the twentieth-century. To some degree, modern ideas and expressions outflowed into early Iranian political nationalism. Owing much to nineteenth and twentieth-century western literature and constituting some progressive advancement vis-à-vis customary writings both in its use of diction and style close to the dialect of regular discourse and in the portrayal of remarkable subjects and topics reflecting individual perspectives and solid contemporary concerns, the idea of modernist writings have been the predominant strain of Persian writing since World War two.

f) The modernist trends: -

When the modernistic trend was used at the beginning of the period of 1960s, Persian literature was meant to be connected with social responsibility, turning into a cognizant literary commitment for Iranian essayists. Meanwhile, they were the same modernist writers who gathered as a group of progressive people supporting the same literary forms, structures and modes of expression for basically similar purposes and confronting traditionalist oppositions viewed as elitist and were not connected, a political power structure viewed as antagonistic and oppressive, and masses apparent as clueless and requiring direction, have constituted since the 1920s an essential Iranian social development. This development has really been uncertain since the First Congress of Iranian Writers was held in Tehran in July 1946, where the writers from all sects were asked to gather and speak about the idea called the language of common people, which included every aspect of society.

During the late 1960s, numerous modernist writers and scholars formally joined the Organisation of Writers of Iran to speak for their rights against the Pahlavi dynasty, fight for their freedom of speech and talk about the flexibility of thought and the press. During September 1968, the unexpected public support of the First Poetry Week of Khusheh Magazine, where more than a hundred poets read from their works, seemed a clear indication that modernist poetry had become a significant voice in Iranian literary life. Through the mid-1970s, the popularity of the weekly magazine Ferdowsi, in whose pages modernist forms of writings, short stories, artistic basic papers, and literary gossip regularly appeared, demonstrated some solidarity in the modernist movement as a non-establishment reformist voice. In June 1977, preceding the popular opposition, people with realistic ideas thought that the Pahlavi dynasty might break down; a large group of people with the modernistic trend raised the question of dissent censorship against the government, mainly the ruling class called the Pahlavi dynasty.

At that point, in October 1977, came the culminating group expression of these modernist writers amid the Pahlavi period with the Ten Nights of Poets and Writers programme, held at the Goethe Institute in Tehran, where more than fifty scholars read from their works during the ten evenings. Very renowned artist and author of fiction Gholam Hussain Sa'edi, activist poet and dramatist Salid Soltanpur, and fiction writer Faridun Tonokaboni, who had been mainly harassed by the Pahlavi dynasty, including imprisonment, were accorded especially warm gatherings by the group of audience. In the opening address, the programme's sponsor, the Organisation of Writers of Iran, avowed as its aim "freedom of thought and the pen," reaffirmed its opposition "to the censorship of books and other printed material in whatever form it might assume and operate under," and requested the suspension of censorship and the disbanding of all government offices and agencies which, contrary to the 1906 Iranian Constitution, were pursuing this course. The situation was heated with respect on the part of participants and the audience that theirs was a significant and dangerous undertaking. With this, people and the association of writers agitated for the Pahlavi rule just to save the basic rights of life[39].

[39.] Faridun Tonokaboni, comp. and ed., Anduh-e Bipayan va Chand Dastan-e Digar, 1st edition, Tehran: Amir-Kabir, 1977.

Modernist writers appeared to be among various identifiable groups at the fore of Pahlavi restrictions in 1978. Consistently that year, these authors may have done minimal creative written work. However, their perspectives were everywhere in print as part of the middle class mass opposition to the Pahlavi dynasty. By the time the king's rule was supposedly ended, it was planned that another political discourse could be started by 1979; it was also mentioned that Iran should think about the new policy, which had not existed earlier during the Shah dynasty. There were so many leading writers, either from the prose section or poetry section, like Mehdi Akhwan Salus, Ahmad Shamlu, Nasim-e-Shumal, Nima Yushiz, etc, who had left the idea of free and modern Iran with no restrictions. Nima Yushij, also known as Nima Yushij, is a pivotal figure in modern Persian literature, credited with founding the "She'r-e No" (New Poetry) movement in Iran. This movement revolutionised Persian poetry, breaking away from classical forms and traditional themes.

Key Aspects of Nima Yushij's Contribution

1. **A Break from Traditional Forms:**

   o Nima Yushij challenged the strict structures of classical Persian poetry, which emphasised formal rhyme and metre schemes. He introduced free verse, allowing for greater flexibility in expression. This approach enabled poets to explore more diverse and personal themes.

2. **Themes and Subjects:**

   o His poetry often focused on contemporary social issues, personal experiences, and emotions. This marked a shift from classical poetry, which was often more abstract and focused on universal themes like love and mysticism. Nima's work gave voice to the common people and addressed the complexities of modern life.

3. **Language and Style:**

   o He employed a more accessible and conversational language, which contrasted with the ornate and elevated diction of traditional Persian poetry. This made his work more relatable to a broader audience.

4. **Symbolism and Imagery:**

   o Nima used rich imagery and symbolism to convey his ideas. His poems often evoke the natural landscape of northern Iran, where he was born, and use these settings to explore deeper emotional and philosophical themes.

5. **Influence and Legacy:**

   o Nima Yushij's influence on Persian poetry is profound. He opened the door for future generations of poets to experiment with form and content, leading to a vibrant and diverse poetic tradition in Iran. His work also reflects a broader trend in world literature towards modernism, where traditional forms were questioned, and new modes of expression were sought.

Critical Reception

➢ **Criticism and Resistance:**

   o Initially, Nima faced significant criticism from traditionalists who viewed his break from classical forms as a betrayal of Persian literary heritage. However, his persistence and the quality of his work eventually gained him recognition.

➢ **Literary Analysis:**

   o Scholars often analyse Nima's work for its innovative use of language, its thematic depth, and its role in reflecting the social and cultural changes in Iran during his time. His poetry is seen as a bridge between classical Persian literature and contemporary Iranian culture.

Nima Yushij's legacy continues to be a subject of study and admiration, representing a crucial turning point in the evolution of Persian literature.

The critique of this regime was mostly discussed throughout their writings, which expressed Iranian views. There were some modern prose writers who were living outside of the country, like Jamalzadeh, Bozorg Alvi, and Sadiq Hedayat. They all struggled to write something good for the future of Iran, but they were mainly not allowed to, so they struggled to express their freedom of speech through their writings, but they failed many times. Iran was in a very bad situation, mainly from 1952 to 1977, because this was the time when the common people of Iran started agitating against the Pahlavi regime.

In any case, by mid-1979, it was clear that these modernist writers were out of venture with the newly formed Islamic Republic of Iran under the leadership of Ruhollah Khomeini. It was the time when Bozorg Alvi Gholam Hasan Sa'edi and some important modernist writers were raising their voices against the fear that they assumed. There was another progressive modern Feminist writer, Simin Danehswar, the most conspicuous lady in Iran, who clearly stated that she would not be nagged once again into a more repressed customary part as a woman. Amid 1981, these modernist writers were in more unstable positions than they had been in through the entire post-Mosaddeq pre-Khomeini period. A letter signed by Baraheni, Daneshvar, Hushang Golshiri, Esma'il Kho'i, Sa'edi, Mohammad' Ali Sepanlu, Shamlu, Soltanpur, and numerous different scholars and different educated people was circulated in June 1981, stating that Khomeini administration outlawing all the periodicals and newspapers, oppression of women, stifling of minority groups, and torture of protesters[40].

Around the same time, Soltanpur was executed by the Iranian government for "a criminal post," "plotting," and "administration in the Sazman-e Cherikha-ye Feda'i-ye Khalq." There were unsubstantiated reports of Ahmad Shamlu's arrest in September and of Baraheni's toward the beginning of November. Afterwards, reports circled that Ahmad Shamlu was hidden by some of his colleagues. Gholam Hasan Sa'edi somehow managed to leave Iran and made arrangements in mid-1982 to distribute another Alefba magazine in France. These modernist writers with progressive approaches were struggling to get their basic rights either in pre-Pahlavi or post-Pahlavi.

Such responses of the Islamic Republic of Iran to the modernist Iranian writers signify the modernist trend in Persian literature as a social movement both during the 1953 to 1978, and Reza Shah Pahlavi period and during the Khomeini period that started in 1979. This was very scary

---

[40.] Aref Qazvini, quoted in Yahya Aryanpur, Az Saba ta Nima, 2 vols. Tehran Ketabha-ye Jibi, 1971.

situation for these modernist trend Persian literature writers that they were failing to manage the significant social impact on new Iran[41].

g) The struggle to start artistic structure for modernism: -

Artistic structures and forms themselves are the first and most inescapable part of modernism in Persian literary works from the formal beginnings of modernism in Nima Yushij's sonnet Afsaneh, published in 1922, and Mohammad' Ali Jamalzadeh's gathering of narrative stories called Yeki Bud Yeki Nabud got published in 1921. This was the actual time when the writers felt that Persian literature put aside the court-supported past of a practice in which types and not individuals were presented, addressed, and depicted and that literature attempted direct communication with the population at large and not just an intellectual middle class. The case of fictional prose during World War II signifies the first phase of modernist development that, somehow, these writers are getting their works recognised. In verse, it was not till the mid-1950s that writers liberated themselves from customary verse designs and started giving their subjects some appropriate literary forms. The Modernist dramatisation became an important art in the 1960s. All through, the past has not been rejected in its essence in its own context but only as not deserving imitation merely out of respect. Also, it was largely discussed that there has been great conflict between traditionalists and modernists; some of the modernist writers have argued that there is a connection between traditional literary forms, subjects and advocates and the traditional, oppressive political power structure that many modernists have felt it was their major duty to fight.

Many issues have been discussed in the context of modernist writers. Some of them are the resistance to the Pahlavi government, dismissal of parts of Shi'i organisations and practices, concern with affirmed financial and social backwardness in Iran, the complete assurance of Iranian tradition with new approaches with articulation of a feeling of culture-particular distance or loss of Iranian roots, and a feeling of strong social and cultural nationalism.

---

[41]. Ibid.

The modernist writers saw themselves during the post-Mosaddeq, which was not recurring the strong voice for the Iranians ahead. Some liberal writers like Bozorg Alavi and Behazin have been against Pahlavi since the beginning of World War II. This was the time Jalal actually started writing complete explicit or implicit criticism of the Pahlavi dynasty. Ahmad Shmalu has been a consistent stand against the Pahlavi dynasty, even if the system tried to influence him through poetic symbolism. In the 1960s, Gholam Hasan Saédi was one of the eminent writers who fictionalised indictments of Iranian society and culture. Furthermore, the short story author and folklorist Samad Behrangi had very strong messages about adult Iranian society and culture for readers of his children's stories. Numerous modernists paid for their feedback with detainment, among them Baraheni, Beh'azin, Mahmud Dowlatabadi, Gholam Hasan Sa'edi, and Soltanpur. The Pahlavi regime's corruption, inefficiency, and excessive dependence upon the West led Iran to a different and critical condition. The annihilation of customary town culture and settling of the village people and their clans, infringement of the 1906 Iranian Constitution, oversight, political suppression, and the operation of SAVAK were foci of consideration of these reformist authors[42].

h) An analytical understanding of the contemporary writers: -

Iran was the country where Islam deepened its roots in the section called the Criticism of Aspects of Shi'i Islam. For instance, Jalal-Al-e Ahmad's "Eftar-e Bimowqe" (The Untimely Breaking of the Fast, 1945) relates the naughty, legitimate way a lower middle class bazaar operator can break his Ramazan fast quickly, the story mocking the religious directions and remarking on how powerful the manages of religious leaders are for everything except the education. Sadeq Chubak's "Ba'd az Zohr-e Akhar-e Pa'iz" (An Afternoon in Late Autumn, 1945) contrasts a teacher's request that a student learn Arabic supplications by heart and the lower class students' troublesome life that no measure of mastery in Arabic will improve. In Nader Naderpur's popular short poem called "Qom," that religious centre is depicted as sterilised and

---

[42.] Richard Cottam, Nationalism in Iran (Pittsburgh, University of Pittsburgh, 1964; expanded edition, 1979); Leonard M. Helfgott, "The Structural Foundations of the National Minority Problem in Revolutionary Iran," Iranian Studies 13 (1980):

dead. Ebrahim Golestan focuses on and around societal hypocrisy for the sake of religion in Safar-e-Esmat (Esmat's Journey,1965), a story in which a whore repenting her past through a pilgrimage to a religious hallowed place is welcomed by a Mollah who approaches her there to end up one of his so-called sisters of the holy place and minister to the requirements of male travellers (by method for legitimate, transitory sigheh marriages) a temporary marriage agreement also known as having a concubine is one of Shi'ism's most controversial regulations. What has been traditionally defined in the category of sigheh in Iran is the possibility that it provides religious families who restrict their children in their interaction with the opposite gender. In an important 1960s poem called "Arusak-e-Kuki" (The Wind-up Doll), premier Iranian poetess Farough Farrokhzad describes the life she implies numerous Iranians live in these words:

I desire you, although I know

I shall never embrace you

You embody the bright blue sky

I remain a mere caged bird.

Full of desire,

From behind cold bars, I look at you

And hope one day, a hand would

Set me free to fly to you.

A neglectful moment can occur

When I fly out of this silent cell

Laugh at the watchful eyes of the guard

And begin a new life beside you[43].

There were so many persistent anti-Shi'i animus in imaginative literary works consisting of different ideals, at the very least. Where anti-clericalism

---

[43] A translation form of Forough Farrokhzad, by Iraj bashiri Retrieved from the given site, http://www.angelfire.com/rnb/bashiri/Poets/Forugh.html.

and the rejection of many folk Shi'i practices were discussed, it appears to additionally include a xenophobic dismissal of Islam as an Arab assault on Iranian culture. Prominent poet Mehdi Akhwan Salus, for instance, refers to Islam in his famous poem "Akhar-e Shahnameh" (The Ending of the Shahnameh,1957) as "false lights" that showed up the prospect at the end of the Sasanian era.

Some of the writers like Sadiq Chubak dismiss religion as insane, while Jalal-Al-e Ahmad argues for a change of Islam today so it may satisfy the decent and applicable ethical quality it showed in the distant past. It is a position similar to the division, made well known by Ali Shari'ati, between Safavid Shi'ism and 'Alavid Shi'ism.'

A theme which Jalal-Al-e Ahmad asserts is a piece of the motivation behind his novel Nun-va- Qalam (The Letter' N' and the Pen,1961), Alavid Islam is the pure, honourable Shi'i faith practiced in Ali's day. Safavid Shi'ism is the narrative of the religion during recent centuries from the time it compromised with the Safavid state, whenceforth people paid lip service to Shi'i heroism but were no longer willing to be heroic themselves that some of the practices of Muslims followed by Shi'i have been criticised and condemned by modernist authors[44].

Iranians had difficulty with much of its attribution to the influence of Shi'ism in their daily life, which is a third thematic sphere of consideration in modernist Persian literary works. Financial hardship and numbness are portrayed in story after story. This can also be seen in Sadiq Chubak's Sang-e-Sabur (The Patient Stone,1966), which mainly talks about the desperate lives of characters; such themes are also presented in many stories. The consequence of such severe neediness and hardship is a kind of social destitution, as indicated by the result of such oppressive poverty and deprivation is a sort of cultural poverty; in a critique on Jalal-Al-e-Ahmad's "Bacheh-ye-Mardom" (Someone Else's Child, 1948), a typical story in this regard,

---

[44] Jalal Al-e Ahmad, Karnameh-ye Seh Saleh (Tehran: Ketab-e Zaman, 1967), cites religion, language, and literature as cultural factors determining his personality as an Iranian. Idem, Khasi dar Miqat (Tehran: Nil, 1964), pp. 105-106, sees cultural iden-tity as determined by language, culture and tradition(s).

Where Jalal-Al-e-Ahmad targets the society for its social causes,

One should always consider their day-by-day bread

as improvements and nothing more. Furthermore, certainly,

the individual who endures to the marrow of his or her

bones from neediness scarcely contemplates such enhancements.

Furthermore, society has presented this neediness on these individuals,

Not simply material neediness but rather social

neediness and passionate destitution. The

prime offender was a misinformed and deluding society,

a general public that was topsy-turvy from its first block[45].

i) The Attributes of Westernisation by the Various Writers: -

The Pahlavi regime apparently observed western-style modernisation. The modernisation was a response to the monetary and social hardship that portrays the lives of the vast majority of Iranians. Actually, the idea of westernisation has always been of great concern, which is a serious threat to Iranian culture and identity, according to various modernist Iranian scholars and writers. Syed Md Ali Jamalzadch has always talked portrayal of Iranian students coming back from France in "Farsi Shekar ast" Persian Is Sweet, 1921, down to the counter-colonialist and anti-American rhetoric of Ahmad Shamlu, Gholam Hasan Sa'edi, and others in 1978 and later, the risks for Iran and their people for their culture have always been discussed by the modernist writers that how the western life has become part of Iranian culture and has become in day to day routine.

For instance, Gholam Hasan Sa'edi is seen as especially delicate to the risk of westernisation. One of his works, named Gav: The Cow in 1969, speaks against the westernisation setting of a town which is mainly built the representation of western culture. There have been so many dramas and plays written on the same theme, which clearly show the corruption evolving

---

45. Ibid.

in Iranian society. Gholam Hasan Saédi speaks about the corrupt system in Iran in his work "Dandil," the title story in a 1966 collection where a teenage virgin high school girl is brought to a decrepit red-light area by her father. He tries to sell her to the pimps in the neighbourhood., Others, including the corrupt cop who offers her to an American armed force sergeant close to the army area where the prostitution was under the curtain. In this story, Gholam Hasan Saédi talked about the innocence of Iran, that a girl was forced to sleep with an American army man, and when he spends the night with the girl, he leaves in the morning without paying for anything. This is how the Americans used to exploit the Iranians with the help of the Iranian Government, who never bothered to think about the future of Iran. The writers of that time naturally concurred that Iranians cannot reject the advances and the technologies merely because they are western. However, in this modern and industrialised world, Iran must stand up and make changes in society. There had been mixed feelings as well that this should not be at the cost of Iranians' life and their culture. Iran has always been in the transitional phase. During the 7th Century, it had to bear with the Arabs who attacked Iran and forced them to change their culture according to Islam. So, Iran has always had some very problematic situations since the Sasanian time, where it can be seen in Ferdowsi's Shahnameh[46].

Jalal-Al-e Ahmad, in his work Nefrin-e-Zamin (The Cursing of the land,1968), cites the exact corrupt system of a teacher's account of a year in a Persian village during the early 1960s. The story particularly criticises the Pahlavi government's land redistribution, the mechanisation of agriculture, provincial state-funded training, and military induction, all of which pertain

---

[46.] Naser Mo'azzen,comp., Dah Shab: Shabha-ye Sha'eran va Nevisandegan dar An joman-e Farhangi-ye Iran va Alman (Tehran: Amir Kabir, 1978). Cassette tapes of the whole program, including extemporaneous remarks, ap-plause, and the like, were distributed later by the New York-based Committee for Artistic and Intellectu-al Freedom in Iran. As for the earlier milestones in modernist Persian literature as a social movement, the proceedings of the First Congress of Iranian Writers were published as Nakhostin Kongreh-ye Nevisandegan-e Iran (Tehran: Iran--USSR Society, 1947; reprinted, 1979), 303 pp. At one point in his statement to the Congress, Communist fiction writer Bozorg 'Alavi (b. 1904) declared: "Writers are leaders of the people [qowm] and should know how to lead the society [ja-me'eh]"l (p. 183). On the founding of the Organization of Iranian Writers, according to Ferdowsi, no. 881 (22 Mehr 1968): 21, there were about eighty members of Kanun-e Nevisandegan-e Iran by mid-1968, the year the organization was founded. Also in Ferdowsi, no. 888 (11 Azar 1968): 19, under the title "Bahsi darbareh-ye Nevisandeh va Azadi," the Organization's first general meeting is described. The proceedings of the First Poetry Week of Khusheh Magazine were published as Yadnameh-ye Nakhostin Hafteh-ye She'r-e Khusheh, comp. and ed. Ahmad Shamlu (Tehran: Khusheh, 1969). The public support of the event is described in "Shab-ha-ye She'r-e Khusheh," Ferdowsi, no. 878 (1 Mehr 1968):

to the central social problem of the community's loss of roots as the feudal, agrarian; these were the ground level problems cited and brought up to the Iranians people that how Pahlavi regime took side to the western government without thinking the pros and cons of their own people. Mehdi Akhavan-e Sales treats two other aspects of this rootlessness in his popular poems "The Ending of the Shahnameh" and "Shush-ra-Didam" 1972). He mainly tries to explain that people should not leave their roots because separation leads people nowhere, and man just cannot leave people thinking about society and their culture. He further explains that self-conscious Iranians are thus dreamers in a world they cannot control and do not understand or fit into. They are living, as it were, after their time. Later on, in another story named Golestan's novel, Asrar-e Ganj-e Darreh-ye Jenni (Secrets of the Treasure of the Haunted Valley), talks about how rootlessness is part of the point to a villager whose sudden wealth turns him into an individual unable to control himself in obtaining things from the big city which, back in the village, contribute to the destruction of traditional life there. The story is a political and moral story as well, insofar as the villager whose sudden, undeserved wealth and subsequent superficial modern ways, together with an inevitable entourage of sycophantic and greedy followers, seems paralleled by Reza Shah Pahlavi and his regime, which Golestan is damning for foolish, superficial, and culture destroying westernisation. The critique was made up of almost every modernist writer, who cited tiny examples of their surroundings. The one and most important feature that needs to be discussed is basically social and cultural nationalism[47].

Social and Cultural nationalism is graphically inferred in many contemporary composition writings through the depiction of Iranian social history, local colour, territorial traditions, dialects, etc. There was a time when Reza Pahlavi banned the wearing of the chador shrouds. The return of a climate in the Islamic Republic of Iran that coerces women to wear chadors makes such a story, which Jalal-Al-e Ahmad narrates in his different works.

The turmoil in Iranian life during World War II is reasonably portrayed in Jalal-Al-e Ahmad's Tajhiz-e Mellat (The Mobilisation of Iran, 1946), which

---

[47.] Jalal Al-e Ahmad, Karnameh-ye Seh Saleh (Tehran: Ketab-e Zaman, 1967), p. 164, cites religion, language, and literature as cultural factors determining his personality as an Iranian. Idem, Khasi dar Miqat Tehran, 1964.

gives the reader a vibe for the disappointment, vulnerability, and different responses of lower working-class urban Iranians to the Allied Occupation that started in 1941. Gholam Hasan Sa'edi's various plays and short stories of the 1970s give readers a tangible vibe for different, ordinary towns and urban conditions, as well as their critical living style. His most renowned story, The Cow, graphically speaks to town life, superstitions, fatalism to the inevitable, and attentiveness of rural Iran. All the writers of that time had different opinions about the Khomeini. It had been seen that Khomeini also got criticised by the modernist frame of work only because of the idea of an Islamized republic. The Pahlavi dynasty had many things to say, but their policy, which was made by so many clerics, was against the philosophy of free liberal Iran.

j) Perspective of the contemporary writers: -

There are many Persian writings and books, particularly short stories mainly from and during the Reza Shah time, which have shown the complete depiction of Iranian life and their social, cultural, and economic conditions. This is how it can be perceived that Iranian culture often is the unavoidable shading and specificity of literary settings, which suggests profound established and intense connections with respect to the authors of the region. This implies the writers of the contemporary world depict the exact cultural scenario of that time, focusing on the political agendas as well.

Modernist writers of Persian literature were required to embody a lot of political culture with their patriotism. Mainly, the modernist Iranian writers who have been an essential centre of Iranian intellectuals for the greater part of the contemporary world for a long and who have constituted the one section of Iranians personally acquainted with the West and western thoughts, including political patriotism, should presumably be the frontline of nationalist expression in Iran. Another aspect which can also be seen in this context is that the modernist Persian writers with their writings have been from half-a-century ago, meanwhile inside Iran, it was adopted to connect with the idea called realism to engage its reflecting contemporary social and cultural issues within the reach of the writers. It was mainly projected to speak about the present exploitation taking place in the different parts of Iran, mainly in the capital of the country[48].

The rise of modernist Persian literature in the early years of the century is assumed to have had direct links with nationalist sentiments and aspirations, as the word "nation" joined "God," "king," and "beloved" as an object of address in verse, and as the new literary forms and diction that have become hallmarks of the modernist tradition developed precisely because writers felt it their responsibility to speak, not to a literary elite, but to all of the people, educating and moulding them into participants in modern society. This was one of the beauties of the writings that have been used during the entire revolution period.

Most importantly, political patriotism itself won't be as normal a standard for these authors to rally and bring together behind as is often supposed. It has demonstrated no simple issue for contemporary Iranian writers either to characterise the constituent elements of an Iranian national community or to marshall nationalistic dedication to existing or proposed institutions of that Iranian group. For instance, on the issue of the constituent elements of Iranianness, Jalal-Al-e Ahmad insists on the Persian language, Persian-Iranian culture, and Shi'i Islam as fundamental ingredients[49].

According to Simin Daneshvar, Jalal-Al-e Ahmad's remedy of Shi'i Islam as a necessary part of Iranian identity was the result of learning and understanding somehow, Jalal-Al-e Ahmad had a great experiment with Marxism, socialism, and to some extent, existentialism, and his relative get back to religion and the Hidden Imam was both a means of preserving national identity, as well as a path toward human dignity, mercy, justice, reason and virtue. Jalal-Al-e Ahmad had a need for such a religion where humanity could be served at its best. After all, he was one of those writers

---

[48] The reformist character of most of modernist Persian literature is discussed in Michael Hillmann, "Reza Baraheni: A Case Study of Politics and the Writer in Iran, 1953-1977,11 Major Voices in Contemporary Persian Literature, Literature East & West 20 (1976): 304-313; idem, "Book Review: An Anthology of Modern Persian Poetry (1978)," Major Voices, pp. 314-318; and Gert J. J. de Vries, "Book Review: The Little Black Fish," Major Voices,

[49] Jalal Al-e Ahmad, Karnameh-ye Seh Saleh (Tehran: Ketab-e Zaman, 1967), p. 164, cites religion, language, and literature as cultural factors determining his personality as an Iranian. Idem, Khasi dar Miqat (Tehran: Nil, 1964), pp. 105-106, sees cultural iden-tity as determined by language, culture and tradition(s).

who believed that realism must be taken to the ground level so that society could understand the problems as well as the pros and cons[50].

However, Jalal-Al-e Ahmad failed to win the support of others among contemporary writers. Among them, just American-prepared poetess Tahereh Saffarzadeh states Shi'i Islam is the sole salvation of Iran from the Pahlavi. No man's land was clearly portrayed by Sadiq Chubak and Farough Farrokhzad in their particular self-portraying lyrics entitled "Ah-e Ensan" (The Sigh of Mankind,1945) and "Ay Marz-e Porgohar (O Jewel-studded land 1966)." Meanwhile, Jala Al-e Ahmad's position, not to speak of Tahereh Saffarzadeh's, would be rejected out of hand, one can guess, by Mehdi Akhavan Sales, Samad Behrangi, Sadiq Chubak, Ahmad Shamlu, and many others.

With respect to the Persian dialect as a fundamental segment of Iranians, such Azarbayjani writers as Samad Behrangi, Sa'edi, etc could barely share that view, regardless of whether they recognise that Persian is the most widely used language of Iran. Furthermore, Jalal-Al-e Ahmad's uncommon inclination for his own Persian-Iranian social legacy as a fundamental segment of Iranian personality is not something shared by at least a large minority of the Iranian population. The very expression "Persian-Iranian" (fars in Persian) is an update that the Persian writing of Iran cannot be expected to involve an Iranian national writing. On the other hand, there may not be a solid or significant Iranian socio-political arrangement in which a putative Iranian writing would make an appearance. The familiar facts of the great ethnic and linguistic diversity in Iran, the diversity of lifestyles in villages, towns, cities, and the capital, the great diversity in exposure to education, modern ways, and the outside world, the gap between the lifestyles of the poor and the wealthy, and the extremely fluctuated states of mind toward conventional esteems and change are for the most part hindrances to a mutual social, or political feeling of Iranianness[51].

In this great heterogeneity, the Persian-Iranian writers are speaking for and from the dominant Persian-Iranian culture, which is something other

---

[50] Simin Daneshvar, "Ghorub-e Jalal,Yadnameh-ye Jalal," Arash 21, no. 31, New Series 6 (September/October 1981): 47; reprinted in idem, Ghorub-e Jalal (Tehran: Revaq, 1982), pp. 29-30.

[51] Richard Cottam, Nationalism in Iran (Pittsburgh, Uni-versity of Pittsburgh, 1964; expanded edition, 1979); Leonard M. Helfgott, "The Structural Foundations of the National Minority Problem in Revolutionary Iran," Iranian Studies 13 (1980): 195-214.

or less than speaking as an Iranian. In nutshell the modernist Iranian writers may not have had a common sense of community that could be the basis for group feeling and action or for reacting as a group to the monarchy's twin government nationalist projects of cultural assimilation to and Pahlavism.

In the meantime, the writers who believed in producing something in or as some nationalistic ideas were a natural and significant feature of the ideologies of most modernist writers in the pre-revolution, pre-Khomeini period; a significant number of these writers must have hesitated to express their views directly since the very kind of patriotism they upheld was being proclaimed as official Pahlavi regime ideology. At the end of the day, passionate advocacy in literary works of a secular, modernist Persian-Iranian nationalism might have been interpreted by numerous readers as support for the very views that the unfriendly Pahlavi regime was upholding. But a more important problem lies here. For the most part, modernist Iranian writers and the Pahlavi state actually shared a basic ideology of material progress, modernisation without becoming western, and Persian-Iranian political nationalism. The modernist writers tried to make Iran a modernised country but tried to skip through westernisation. Writings have always been impactful and advisable to Iranian society[52].

k) The importance of pre-Islamic culture and its convention:-

The importance of pre-Islamic Iranian culture and convention, equal rights for Iranian women, a diminishment in the impact of Shi'i Moslem leaders and practices, and the requirement for Iran to take part completely in the world beyond its borders were other aspects of the views shared by most modernist writers and officially by the Pahlavi regime. Both these writers and the Pahlavi regime declared the need for Iran and Iranians to make the best utilisation of the West, its thoughts, technologies, and products without losing Iranian identity in the process. On account of the administration,

---

[52] Nikki R. Keddie, "Iran: Change in Islam; Islam and Change," International Journal of Middle Eastern Studies 11 (1980): 534, describes the situation in these words: In somewhat different ways the Pahlavi regime and most of its intellectual critics were aggressively secularist. Both shared in the glorification of pre-Islamic Iran, though the Shahs stressed the great dynasties while radical critics looked to the "communist" heretic Mazdak, until recently both accepted fairly wholesale Westernization, with a stress on large, modern industry, Western fashions, consumer goods, and fads. Both tended to look down on the 'ulama and the traditionalist classes as remnants of an old way of life that would surely disappear through secularization and modernization.

economics caused things to get out of hand by the 1970s. In the case of the writers, however much they waged verbal war on Jalal-Al-e Ahmad's Gharbzadegi (Westoxication), so, somehow or somewhere, Iranians tried to adopt the idea of westernisation but not at the cost of their culture and civilisation[53].

The writers of the contemporary world were the most Western-oriented among intellectuals in the arts and humanities; the very forms of their art and the very ideas of their roles were inspired by, or at least impacted by, western models. The significance they attached to the rowshanfekr (intellectual) class and to intellectual approaches to things have been western. The modernist writers supported an essentially secular social and political order, which seemed to represent the effects of their exposure to western ideas. In respect, they have displayed a similar kind of elitism that was part of the myopia that caused the downfall of the Pahlavi regime. This was very natural; as artists, dramatists and writers of fiction, and not social and political thinkers, there was little reason for them not to be innocent. Further, it had no personal political experience for over twenty-five years during the Khomeini regime and Reza Shah Pahlavi dynasty.

These modernist writers were literally thwarted or co-opted by the Reza Shah regime and ill-equipped to provide social or political direction to their followers. They were critical, doubtful, sceptical, and warred among themselves as much as with societal problems. It is hardly surprising that modernist Persian literature is primarily a literature of unhappy endings. Or, then again, when the endings are not disastrous, they regularly include the telling determination of the plot through the protagonist's withdrawal or escape from the circumstance that constituted the story conflict. Other than various poems and stories that Sadique Hedayat subject's themes of the individual wishing had never been conceived or seeking a death that refuses to free one from life, the modernist Persian writing is overflowing with social and political clashes from which even the most thoughtful characters, in the long run, remove themselves by leaving the contentions and what has all the earmarks of being Iran behind. This is the reason that

---

[53] The most popular writing on the subject is Al-e Ahmad's polemic Gharbzadegi (1962), available till near the end of the Pahlavi era only in underground editions. For more, see the chapters on Gharbzadegi in Michael Hillmann, comp. and ed., Iranian Society: An Anthology of Writings by Jalal Al-e Ahmad, Lexington, Kentucky: Mazda, 1982.

modernist writers have always been appreciated due to the closeness of reality.

For instance, if someone has to understand the actual incidents in Bushehr in 1922, one must read Sadiq Chubak's novel *Tangsir* (1963), which is the dramatic story of a Tangestani who is frustrated in his attempts to seek redress against four Bushehr notables who have cheated him and who thus takes justice into his own hands, assassinates the four, and after that tries to escape Iran by boat with his wife and child. One of the important novels by Jalal-Al-e Ahmad, *The Letter "N" and the Pen*, is a once-upon-a-time symbol of a religiously inspired revolution that expels an oppressive ruler and his corrupt and sycophantic regime from the nation. However, once the revolutionaries are in power, it becomes obvious that only their pioneer is propelled by religious standards. Ultimately, the revolution fails because of this and because of the stubbornness and selfishness of the people at large. Some revolutionaries got back to the monarchy when it returned to power. Some are executed. Others, including one of the two major characters, escape to India. The other major character left their family members in that very situation alone to struggle with their destiny. The situation was so messed up during that time. In this way, Nader Ibrahimi can also be read throughout his story 'Bad-e Mehregan' is a third kind of illustration where the political activism of University of Tehran students leading up to the June 1963 demonstrations is depicted where one can understand the frustration level against this monarchy where no one had right to dissent with the government ideology. The literature tried to bring up all the situations which made them feel unsafe and insecure in their own country and land. Freedom of expression was not guaranteed, and people were not free to do so; even their education was decided by the upper regime.

This has also been seen in Syed Md Ali Jamalzadeh's collection 'Yaki bud wa Yaki nabud' Once-Upon-a-Time collection (1921), where it was perceived that the representation of lack of social direction, dedication or purpose within or among different Iranian groups has been part of modernist (Persian literature) since its beginnings. For instance, one of the short stories,' Farsi Shekaar ast' (Persian Is Sugar), also represents the earlier described heterogeneity of Iranian culture and society. Syed Md Ali Jamalzadeh describes a group of Iranians detained by government officials in a Customs House cell. Each of the four detained individuals is exceptionally worried about his plight. But, in response to questions by a young villager from nearby, who is the least sophisticated of the group, an Iranian student just back from France hides behind abstract French nouns that he includes in every Persian utterance. And a Mollah retreats to Arabic religious saws. Indeed, even the storyteller, who depicts himself as world-wise and sensible, does not think to address the group to see if they might not collectively figure a way out of their predicament. Jamalzadeh very intelligently tried to depict the situation that occurred in Iran during the revolution period through his writings.

In the very different medium of satiric drama the story of Iran's salvation, is what Forough Farrokhzad depicts through the mouth of the little girl in her famous poem called "Kasi keh Mesl-e Hichkas Nist" (Someone Who Is Like No One, 1966). This also can be seen in the Ahmad Shamlu's famous poem "Pariya" (The fairies) in 1953.

The hoped-for hero in Forough Farrokhzad's poem is a single individual who will set things right and try to build up a just society. The Ahmad Shamlu also had similar story though he tried to build a society where people can think without any turbulences.

One can scarcely accuse these modernist writers for lack of prescience in any case, the certainties that they never showed the cohesiveness that they in their works indict Iranian society for not showing, that they chose not to take great risks individually or severally for the most part, in short, that they did not display the courage that other groups demonstrated in 1978, while they all were looking to have declaring the depths of their commitment to social change prompt lingering questions about the level of their engagement. It has also been seen that these writers mainly claimed for reform, not revolution. But the fact could not deny that the whole idea was to change the social structure of Iranian society[54].

But, it needs to be added that even if these writers had been both perceptive and political, it is doubtful that they would have been particularly

---

[54] The reformist character of most of modernist Persian literature is discussed in Michael Hillmann, "Reza Baraheni: A Case Study of Politics and the Writer in Iran, 1953-1977,11 Major Voices in Contemporary Persian Literature,Literature East & West 20 (1976): 304-313; idem, "Book Review: An Anthology of Modern Persian Poetry (1978)," Major Voices, pp. 314-318; and Gert J. J. de Vries, "Book Review: The Little Black Fish," Major Voices.

influential through their writing. In light of the thematic thrusts in modernist Persian literature cited above, the social and political direction Iran has taken to date in the post-Pahlavi regime demonstrates the influence of the content of this literature upon Iranian society at large during the later Pahlavi years. Actually, the influence of modernist literature may have raised their voice through their writing skills and tried to bring up the exact scenario of Iran during the Pahlavi regime.

In one of his writings, Jalal-Al-e Ahmad quotes that the

The literature in our country still doesn't constitute

an occupation. It is more of a diversion. The days

when a poet or writer sought refuge at some imperial

the court is gone. But in its place, an audience of the

the general public has not yet taken the writers into

their arms, there are still writers who print 200

copies of their works paid out of their own pockets.[55]

Jalal-Al-e Ahmad's magnum opus, Gharbzadegi, is the complete depiction of Iran's socio, cultural and political situation during the Reza Shah regime. Modernist writers always had a tough time managing and maintaining the scenario of literature where everything was bound to be banned in every circumstance.

In view of some literature, the modernist literary figures faced a dilemma during the pre-Khomeini period. Things, including their effectiveness as a social movement, may now be changing. First, a number of writers, having been politicised during 1978, may abandon the modes and stances of their 1953-1977 activity that they were non-political and, with the real political experience they have recently acquired, participate more knowingly in the social and political change process. Second, these modernist, secular,

---

55. Al-e Ahmad, „Chand Nokteh," pp. 62-63. The situation had not changed by the 1970s, according to Faridun Tonokaboni, Mardi dar Qafas, 2nd ed. (Tehran, 1972), pp. 88-89,

nationalist writers are finally defined as a group ideologically opposite a natural inimical group, the Islamic Republic of Iran[56].

The point in saying that modernist writers are now pitted against the natural enemy of people of their intellectual orientation and that these writers will behave more instinctively and cohesively is that the nationalist banner is now in their hands alone, as well as the banner of non-Islamic Iranian traditions. When Ruhollah Khomeini called the dismissal of Abolhasan Banisadr from the Presidency of the Islamic Republic the final victory of the Republic over nationalism, he demonstrated how clearly lines on this issue are drawn. These writers also, vis-à-vis a religious state that naturally is not inclined to give individuals freedom of choice in religious and moral matters, can again champion individual rights. They are again the champions of modernisation, progress, and the like, with no monarch this time to steal their rhetorical thunder. It was assumed that now, a true test in Iranian society of the potential appeal of such orientations will be conducted, with no Pahlavi state to impose modernism, modernisation, and modernity from above. Obviously, this regular arrangement of traditionalist and fascist political forces versus modernist intellectuals is no guarantee that modernist Persian literature will have any more prominent social impact in the future, either in the Pahlavi time or the Khomeini time frame for there remains the reality of the constrained size of the audience of this writing's group. In this manner, any potential noteworthy effect will be in the long haul. This implies a long time of proficiency and state-funded instruction programmes, combined with concerted efforts at opening readers' eyes to ideas beyond the ideology of the Islamic republic, years before those millions of people who cast their oral votes in the streets of Tehran in 1978 would vote differently. And the Reza Shah regime was about to finish with this drastic change in Iran.

[56.] Fergus M. Bordewich, "Fascism without Swastikas: Mis-reading the Iranian Revolution," Harper's (July 1980), 65-71.

Persian Literature and Its Social Impact on the Iranian Revolution 1979.

a) The Impact of Persian Literature: -

Modern Persian Literature pertains to writings from the twentieth-century, and as that century drew to a close and the present one commenced, critics have begun to show a lively interest in the literature of this period. Major new studies from markedly different points of view have been published. The present work makes the author's standpoint clear, although the subtitle is somewhat misleading because by no means does the book cover all the literature of the past century. Nevertheless, Kamran Talattof has proposed a new and innovative approach to the understanding of modern Persian literature. This he calls "episodic literary movement," a theory that brings political and social conditions into sharp focus. Briefly, he argues that political and social conditions at any given time produce a pertinent "ideology of representation" and that this ideology helps to shape, and is shaped by, a cluster of "aesthetically significant literary texts" that constitute a "literary episode." Ideology is related to literature through a shared set of metaphors. The history of Persian literature is conventionally viewed as an integrated continuum. Because of the impact of ideology on the production of literature, the author defines the literary history of the modern period as a "series of distinct episodes distinguishable by their ideology of representation. Thus, the literary history of this period moves by "episodes," and these constitute, in effect, a new form of periodisation. Closely paralleling social movements are "literary movements," and the author finds four of these in twentieth-century literature: "Persianism" in the early part of the century, "Marxist-oriented" Committed Literature" in the decades before the 1979 revolution, "Islamic Literature after 1979(on the decline after the mid-1990s), and "Post-Revolutionary Women's Literature." The focus on separate literary episodes helps make clear how metaphors form connections between them. For example, the author discusses the changing significance of the events at Karbala for the "Persianist" writers, the committed writers, and the producers of Islamic literature. Likewise, he points out how the writers of Islamic literature in the early 1980s appropriated and redefined much of the imagery and rhetoric of the committed writers, although the two groups were ideologically opposed. The present theory works for the period surveyed, a period defined by two revolutions and dominated by active social change and popular political involvement. Would it work as well for the period from the rise of the Timurids to the end of the Safavids, for example? In other words, is this a theory tailor-made for the twentieth-century, or can it be generalised to the larger field of Persian literary history? Finally, Talattof eschews" the ethics of self-expression "in favour of literature's being "a powerful social and collective reaction to prevailing social conditions." There is much evidence in the period in question that both forces were at work[57].

If Syed Mohammad Ali Jamalzadeh (1892 – 1997) is considered the inaugurator of modern Persian prose fiction writing and Nima Yushij (1897 – 1960) is considered the father of modern Persian poetry writer in the early twentieth-century, then it must be noted down in mind that their works were preceded by the efforts of other fiction writers, poets, and playwrights in the late nineteenth-century. When scholars look at the magnum opus of Ibrahim Beig, Siyahatnameh-ye-Ibrahim Beig (The Travel Memoirs of Ibrahim Beig), a bridge between the dominant nineteenth-century prose genre of the safarnameh (travel memoirs) and twentieth-century fiction, as well as at the poetry of Mirzadeh Eshqi (and others) and the closet plays of Mirza Aqa Tabrizi before and during the Iranian constitutional revolution (1906 – 11), demonstrates that, in contrast to traditional Persian writing, the early modernists veered toward literature of social and political criticism[58].

[57.] The discussion of twentieth-century Persian prose fiction, see Hassan Kamshad, Modern Persian Prose Literature (Cambridge: Cambridge University Press, 1966); and M. R. Ghanoonparvar, Prophets of Doom: Literature as a Socio-political Phenomenon in Modern Iran (Lanham, MD: University Press of America, 1984). On the development of modern Persian poetry, see Ahmad Karimi-Hakkak, Recasting Persian Poetry: Scenarios of Poetic Modernity in Iran (Salt Lake City: University of Utah Press, 1995). On Iranian drama, see M. R. Ghanoonparvar and John Green, eds., Iranian Drama: An Anthology (Costa Mesa, CA: Mazda, 1989). James D. Clark's English translation of Siyahatnameh-ye Ibrahim Beig was published as The Travel Diary of Ibrahim Beig.

[58.] M. R. Ghanoonparvar, "Nava-ye naqqal dar Kelidar" ("The Voice of the Storyteller in Kelidar"), Fasl-e Ketab 2, 1991.

b) Comparative Viewpoints of Various Authors: -

In spite of the fact that the political viewpoint may appear to be more articulated in the works of these writers than in the works of Jamalzadeh and Nima Yushij, the last figures likewise focused on political issues, albeit more obliquely. This also held true for the works of many of the next group of writers, including Sadeq Hedayat and Bozorg Alavi. But In any case, the third era, comprised of writers and poets for example Sadeq Chubak, Jalal-Al-e Ahmad, Ibrahim Golestan, and Ahmad Shamlu, in many ways followed the pattern set by the late nineteenth-century writers, a pattern that to a great extent continued until the Iranian revolution in the works of Forugh Farrokhzad, Gholam hoseyn Sa'edi, Hushang Golshiri, Mahmud Dowlatabadi, and Simin Daneshvar, among others. They were writers who were bringing up the societal framework through their own writing skills.

As far as Iranian cinema (leaving aside famous entertainment movies) is concerned from the 1960s, with the beginning of the alleged new wave, it has been observed a similar commitment to social and political criticism, although the political undercurrent in these films remained veiled due to the existing strict censorship. Such essential movies as *Gav* (*The Cow*, 1969) and *Dayereh-ye mina* (*The Cycle*, 1978) by Daryush Mehrju'i, *Khesht-o a'ineh* (*Brick and Mirror*, 1965) and *Asrar-e ganj-e darreh-yejenni* (*The Secrets of the Treasures of the Haunted Valley*, 1974) by Ibrahim Golestan, *Shazdeh Ehtejab* (*Prince Ehtejab*, 1974) by Bahman Farmanara, *Tangsir* (1973) by Amir Naderi, and *Gavaznha* (*The Deer*, 1976) by Mas'ud Kimia'i offer a couple of cases of the social and political criticism provided by filmmakers[59].

The concentration here, obviously, is on what has been referred to as "intellectual" literature and cinema. However, one could discover comparable political and social engagements in popular fiction and film at the time. With this concise, authentic presentation, it can begin to consider

---

[59] With the international popularity of post-revolutionary Iranian cinema, there have beenincreasing numbers of studies in English, among them, Hamid Dabashi, Close Up:Iranian Cinema, Past, Present, and Future (London: Verso, 2001); and Dabashi, Mastersand Masterpieces of Iranian Cinema (Washington, DC: Mage, 2007); Alberto Elena,The Cinema of Abbas Kiarostami (London: Saqi Books, 2005); Michael J. Fischer, MuteDreams, Blind Owls, and Dispersed Knowledges: Persian Poesis in the TransnationalCircuitry (Durham, NC: Duke University Press, 2004); Hamid Reza Sadr, Iranian Cinema:A Political History (London: I. B. Tauris, 2006); Mehrnaz Saeed-Vafa and JonathanRosenbaum, Abbas Kiarostami (Urbana: University of Illinois Press, 2003); and RichardTapper, ed., The New Iranian Cinema: Politics, Representation, and Identity (London:I. B. Tauris, 2002).

an investigation of the sort of changes, if any, that have happened in post-revolutionary fiction and film.

While the most important contribution of classic Persian literature to the world is the most noteworthy among numerous literature historians and critics, the Persian-Iranian literature of the later period is generally disregarded. Short story writing takes its roots mainly from folklore tales and legend short stories, ancient and classic forms of prose and storytelling, and then due to contact with the Arabic and European writing of the late nineteenth-century. In this period, the impact of western writing on Iranian writers and authors was obvious. New and modern writing techniques are introduced, and few sub-genres have developed exceptionally in the field of short stories. Up to the middle of the nineteenth-century, prose was dominated by traditional folk tales (Hekayat), instructional stories, fairy tales and historic and heroic sagas (Qissa). The start of the twentieth-century is noteworthy as a new period of essential change and modernisation of the literature on a major scale, which opened the route for prose to explore new avenues of expression through which individual thoughts took on a more social hint. Some of the genres received during that period are still prominent in modern Iranian prose, particularly in a short story[60].

Whosoever contributed to the field of setting a new trend in Persian prose writing, Syed Md Ali Jamazadeh is considered the one who broke the rule from traditional to the short story genre in modern Iranian literature. All the previously mentioned writers and scholars concede to similar phases of the development that modern Persian short stories have undergone and experienced. It is mainly divided into three phases: an establishment, a formative period, a period of consolidation and growth, and a period of diversity. The formative period began in 1922 after the publication of Syed Md Ali Jamalzadeh's accumulation of "Yaki Bud wa Yaki Nabud (Once-Upon-a-Time) of short stories Jamalzadeh (1895-1997) spearheaded the class in the Iranian prose and gained its author the name of the "father of the modern Iranian literature." Russian Orientalist K. Chaykin considers,

"Once-Upon-a-Time" is the first work of its kind to imply the techniques of realistic writings, and "the Iranian literature shook off its shoulder

---

[60]. E. Yarshater, Ddstanhii-yi iriTn-i Bastan (Tehran, 1336/1957-58).

the hundreds of years old stories of mystic creatures, lofty and adorned expressions, and framed flowers, birds and butterflies, and at last dared to face with the reality of time[61]."

The collection of Syed Md Ali Jamalzadeh's narrative is pleasant and entertaining and it overflows with sarcastic way and light humour, the most part concentrating on the political issues. It additionally chuckles at the traditions of the Persian culture of the period, exposing to ridicule its backwardness and superstitions. His characters are often from them the common folk, simple, uneducated people.

Jamalzadeh's prose is packed with colloquialisms and proverbial expressions, for he was among the first writers to abandon the ornate artificial style of traditional writing, making simple colloquial language the norm in modem Persian writing. In this way, a new form of narration has arisen in the Iranian literature. It went through merging and development in the framework of folklore, ancient and classical Persian literary heritage, and keeping up with the literary trends and achievements of Europe, particularly France and other literature centres. Creative writers immediately grasped this new short fictional prose narrative. There were numerous admirers of the short story thanks to its beautiful, eloquent and simple language. Exploring different avenues regarding short stories came about not just in the innovation of new forms and approaches but also in the simplification of the Persian language of literature. This was noted as a landmark contribution to modern Persian literature. The beauty of Iranian writers is that they started observing the current order of things with a critical eye and chose social issues such as poverty, bribery, fornication, oppressed women, immorality and hypocrisy of the religious authorities as their main topics[62].

c) The Various Shahs and the European Influence: -

The Nasiruddin Shah, who was the ruler during the Qajar Dynasty, is probably the one who can perceive the constitutional revolution started.

61. Chaykin, K, Concise essay on the modern Persian literature. Moscow: Universitet Trudyashchikhsya Vostoka, 1928.
62. E. G. Browne, A Literary History of Persia, Vol. IV, Cambridge and reprints,1924.

During that time, the zeal for revolution was strengthened with the various changes made because of Nasiruddin Shah's successive treks to Europe and travel to Europe by Iranian immigrants and two excursions to Iran by Syed Jamaluddin Asadabadi when he actively battled against the authoritarian backgrounds. The requirement for corrections to the legislative issues and the efforts of Jamaluddin Asadabadi's devotees had a clear effect on public awakening in Iran. Meanwhile, the progressives and writers (literary world) who had been witness to the physical and spiritual destitution of the country for a long and were anxious about the conditions in Iran and had discovered reasonable grounds to work abroad were the ones who started to educate the people and to train their thoughts by their books and their articles. It is said that Mirza Melkom Khan Isfahani was the one who had influenced the people of Iran and played a very important role in the awakening of their people and spreading the seeds of revolutions throughout the nation as well as "Qanoon" newspaper in London on a later date. His unique and valuable papers reformed the Iranian thought process[63].

Translations of papers and plays by Mirza Fateh Ali Akhoondzadeh, articles and sonnets by Mirza Aqakhan Kirmani, books by Mirza Abdul Rahim Talbof, who taught basics of science and sociology in a simple language, Hajj Zainul Abedin social books, Farsi magazines and papers distributed in Egypt, and the other corner of the country. Businesses were exchanged between Azerbaijan and the Ottoman Empire and Caucasus and, especially during the Japan-Russia war in February 1904, Russia's thrashing from Japan shook the Iranian public opinions; valuable daily papers and magazines in Caucasus and their circulation in Azerbaijan were all components which slowly and at every stage entered into the corrupt social structure of the Iranian social system and warned the so-called elite class in Iran whose archaic bureaucratic system exposed the nation to the danger of prompt occupation by the Russians and English. These were the factors that prepared the people to accept a fundamental revolution; in this way, it can be observed that the disintegrated social system in Iran led to a constitutional revolution[64].

---

[63] YahaiyaAryanpur, AzSaba t Nima (2), Tehran 1372.
[64] Ibid.

Prior to the constitutional revolution and as an introduction to the revolution, numerous scientific, recreational, social and political books were translated about political and social issues and the need to expand modernism.

According to Baqer Momini, who classified his views in a different manner about the culture and social systems of Iran, scientific literature, whose foundations had been laid by the government and the ruling elite, achieved unprecedented growth after Nasiruddin Shah. The political and social literature of the constitutional revolutions were very much trained by the social activists of Iran; this was the time when support came from all sections almost to liberate Iran from the anarchy system. Iran's condition was so bad during the constitutional period that even a single public library was not established; books and schools existed in Europe, whereas in Iran, knowledge was obsolete. It is said that in Iran, one can see pigeon and monkey houses, but there is no public library at all. Later on, social activists questioned how someone could be educated or made aware without basic knowledge. If people were supposedly going to acquire knowledge in European countries and when they got back to their nation, they were badly humiliated. Conditions in Europe differed from those in Iran. In Europe, facilities exist for learning, whereas in Iran, no such institutions exist[65].

d) The Idea Called Freedom from Europe: -

Thus, numerous authors believed that the idea of freedom was conceived in Europe at the same time as the renaissance. This is why it was contrasted with Europe's experience; amid the constitutional revolution, Iran transitioned from poetry to prose. Different slogans in the constitutional literature were made up, and the Travelogue of Ibrahim Beig was taken into consideration so that it could be made up of more progressive themes to respond to the community's desire for modernism. It appeared as though the time of poetry was over, and it belonged to the age of prose now. Some of the writers from different opinions stated that modern prose is doing the same in Iran as it was doing the same thing during the European revolutions in the sixteenth

---

[65.] Jamal, M. رمان. داستان کوتاه. قصه. رمانس. ادبیات داستانی. (Prose: Saga, romance, short story and novel). Tehran: Soxan, this idea discussed in detail, 1961.

and seventeenth centuries. It is said that prose was borne, and poetry was the prevailing format of the past[66].

During the constitutional period in Iran, if a literary text was decided for translation, it should contain such basic subjects as the idea of freedom has always been mentioned inside its context. In spite of the fact that the Qajar sovereigns did not offer credit for such material, Ibrahim Beig's Travelogue or "His Fanatic Blight" by Maragheyi depicts the life of many Iranians who have been taught abroad and, after numerous years, get back to their respective homes, with full of hopes, expectations and enthusiasm. But the moment they get to know and observe the deep gap between the lifestyle of their country and that of the advanced world, which is the West, they get astonished and sick. They fail to understand that all of a sudden, the drastic change from old Iran to Iran with the impact of western colourisations.

The whole scenario was happening in the reign of Reza Shah. After the expulsion of Mohammad Ali Shah Qajar, it has been seen that none of the governments till now were able to take effective steps to amend the administrative structure of the nation or respond to the people's aspirations. Everyone was burnt out of the ongoing circumstance, and all felt that the nation needed a solid centralised government supported by a strong army to rid it of the messy situation[67].

Obviously, in light of the current situation and previously, Reza Shah had shown his actual character and such support was not without any reason. Maybe the most critical explanation behind such help was, to the point that the administration's new aim coincided with literary modernism. During that time, by distributing different magazines and publications, the Iranian intellectuals were trying to hostile such ways of thinking. In fact, all these endeavours were a prelude to the advancement of a particular literary topic which supported novel literature and ended with literature which opposed the current conditions, keeping in mind to represent Reza Shah as a dynamic figure and lover of a strong Iran like that which existed before the birth of Islam.

---

[66] Ibid

[67] E. G. Brown, The Press and Poetry of Modern Persia, Cambridge 1914.

"Magazines such as the Age of Revolution, The Era of revolution, Iran, Vatan (homeland), Free Language, Iran's Kokab (Iran's star), The Voice of Tehran and Tamadon (civilisation) in Tehran and newspapers such as Tajaddod (modernism) in Tabriz, The Jungle and the Red revolution in Rasht, Estakhr, Golestan, Baharestan and Asre Azadi in Shiraz and Rahe Nejat (the way of salvation) and Akhgar (embers) in Isfahan along with publications such as Daneshgah (the university) by Malekolshoara Bahar, Gole Zard by Mirza Yahya Khan, Farhang by Rasht Cultural Association and Azadestan which published only three issues, along with a large quantity of slogans in support of modernism that grieved for Iran's past grandeur and that were even reflected in many of future novels and stories, one way or other supported the new literary theme at the time and justified the special circumstances that put Reza Shah on the throne. Therefore, it must not be surprising to hear from Sepanlu that the Iranian literature from 1921 to 1936, when Hedayat's Blind Owl (Buf-e- Kur) was printed, was wholly erased of politics.[68]"

Until the point when, in 1936, imperialism achieved its peak, Reza Shah's literary jargon engendered a non-political past nationalism. This was the time when Patriotism, Ethics and love of amendments were the leading purposes of the literary themes. In the beginning, even those progressive writers who, in later years, became Reza Shah's bitter critics were captivated by his slogans and published numerous such materials. The political and social conditions during Reza Shah's regime and the mounting censorship and strangulation pushed the literature towards another way. Impacted by western sentimental romanticism historical research, Iranology and romantic stories and epics of bravery became gradually popular in Iran. As a whole, from 1922 to 1941, the dynamic and combatant social literature of the revolution period was exchanged by romantic criticism of individual immoral deeds, and a love of past Iran exchanged a progressive patriotism. This cultural, social, and political writing activity became popular during the period of Reza Shah as well[69].

---

[68] Mohammd Ali Sepanlou, the Article published from University of Tehran, and the idea of Iranian politics was discussed by the writerin detail,1963, from where he graduated.

[69] Abedini, 1987, p.79 رضا عابدینی در کتاب تاریخ طراحی

Regardless of such a political and social environment, various poets and authors began to modernise the literature; however, modernism in literature did not conform with the modernism addressed by Reza Shah's reign. Jamalzadeh has made an effort to comment about some sort of writing in his preface 'Once-Upon-a-Time' about the realism in literature.

He says, "Regretfully departing from the classic literature of the past in Iran is considered destruction of literature, and generally, the same Iranian political despotism that is famous in the world prevails over our literature[70].

Every writer has a different sort of writing skills that is when a writer starts to write she/he addresses only the sages and scholars and does not mind ordinary people at all.

They even neglect to consider many people who have the gift to read and write and can read and understand a simple language. In short, these writers are not after literary democracy. One can conclude that the war between the old and new literature was a sort of clash between an old and outmoded community with a modern community[71].

One of the prominent Iranian writers, Nima Youshij, was born with such a gift whose skill could not fail to mention the exact portrayal of the society's grief, sorrow and pessimism towards their nation. The predominant patriotic sentimental sense was blended with a sense of wrath for cultural deterioration, backwardness, and inflated glorification of the factual and fanciful achievements of ancient Iran. It was the time when Iranians started contradicting European colonialism and meanwhile falling in love with the new European culture, which was accepted by some of the Iranians wholeheartedly.

By the time some of the patriots claimed to be true, they had dissociated themselves from all past traditions, a giant part of Iranian legacy and even Iranian classic poetry. They even felt bad or ashamed of such traditions, yet they were glad for the ancient Iranian civilisation and expressed it in romantic terms. The Iranians were irritated with the European conduct and traditions and were fearful lest the Europeans should look with humiliation at their shape, attire and way of life, but in the meantime, they were proud of

---

[70] Yahaiya Aryanpur p. 433YahaiyaAryanpur, AzSaba t Nima (2), Tehran 1372.
[71] Ibid.

Cyrus, Darius, Anushirvan and the Aryan race. Iranians loved Europe and the European lifestyle but, at the same time, were anti-imperialists. They were both pleased with themselves and resisted themselves. Such a contrast is an expressive picture of the literary genre of that period, which defied the existing conditions.

Before his Blind Owl (Buf-e-kur), which appeared in 1936, Sadeq Hedayat's works easily conformed with nationalism/romanticism themes. His Neyran (1931), Parvin, the Sassan's Daughter (1930), Maziyar (1933), The Last Smile (1933) and his travelogues such as Travel to Isfahan (1932) were influenced by such literature. It was perhaps due to the arbitrary requirements of time that historical novels found much favour in the public eye, and such works flooded the market[72].

Some of the literature needs to differentiate social books and criticism from historical writings. The social books, which had a half-a-century life, were very effective in unveiling the atrocities and crises in contemporary society. Moshfeq Kazemi, Mohammad Hejazi and Mohammad Masood could be referred to in that context. Through such books, which after the First World War had achieved enough progress, these writers depicted the characters of workers and courtesans and criticised their social conditions. Moshfeq Kazemi is considered a pioneer in that field. This is one of the examples of a woman who had been deceived by a rich family and fallen into the gorge of corruption, and under cover of intellectualism, the novel tries to attack the social morals of the times. The personality and performance of Mahin in the 'Horrible Tehran' and 'Ziba' in Mohammad Hejazi's novel can be compared to the writers of that time and found the magnum opus of Mohammad Hejazi.

Therefore, one can say that among Persian novels of the time, like a skillful reporter, Ziba narrates a bureaucracy sans tradition in Iran and a chaotic society after the constitutional revolution[73].

Such an inclination among writers strengthened when the refreshing constitutional atmosphere was clouded and destroyed by the black clouds of the Reza Shahi dictatorship. Since these authors had no means to struggle,

---

[72] Rypka, Jan, History of Iranian Literature, Dordrecht 1968.

[73] Abedini, 1987, p.40رضا عابدینی در کتاب تاریخ طراحی

they magnified the continuous disillusionment in social books. The writer, mainly from that time, was Mohammad Masood. He relates the story of young people whose lives are misused in futile occupations and constant visits to recreational centres and the streets of Share Now (the prostitutes' district in Tehran). He depicts the realities of a community in which the young generation recourse to their last resort, which is suicidal, lonely, fearful and under the pressure of a despotic regime.

According to Abedini: "Influenced by French romanticism, the writer composes a mourning elegy for the poor class, but being ignorant of their inner feelings, he gives a natural tincture to their gloomy and disappointing life[74]."

Anyhow, one should desire to give credit to such novels/books and literary pieces against historical books. This can be understood that the main theme of these works was to display the desires of a new born middle class which wanted rapid change in the society in order to achieve a meritorious rank. The writers of contemporary world focused the inside story of a society through their works. The corruption was gorged with so much of immorality where Iranian considered these activities as out of the culture and civilisation of their own.

e) Some of the Important Literatures Discussed During 1941-1953: -

Nima Youshij was one of the prominent writers who have always been in the limelight for raising their voices against the brutal and corrupt system in Iran. He mentions that I aroused my light while my neighbour came and went on a dark night. He writes that Iran's occupation in September 1941 by the Allied forces was a turning point for contemporary Iranian literature. Iran was possessed by outsiders, meaning foreigners had entered Iran, but against that calamity, the people were relieved and satisfied to see the stupendous forces out of the country. In this way, writers like Nima Youshij ignited their light of expectation. When Reza Shah left Tehran, he articulated their celebration in the following terms:

---

[74] Ibid, Page 43.

When the newspaper vendors were yelling the highlights of the extraordinary supplements about Reza Shah's resignation, for a few moments, I hesitated in utter disbelief. Because the fear of the Shah was so strong in public hearts, and a belief in the continuation of his reign was so firmly established in people that they did not dare to show their joy when they heard the news of their freedom[75].

This was the time when Iran felt liberated from a nightmare of twenty years of hopelessness and gradually started to breathe again. The leaders and the activists who aroused their voices during the Reza Shah regime were freed, the nation's politics started to breathe a little, and freedom of speech and writing was expanded in newspapers and political and guild associations. During these twelve years, Iran had a decent opportunity to practice its own democracy. Clash of opinions, dynamism, and activity in every field, public protest, political and intellectual formations, variety of thoughts, attacks, arrests and executions were the special features of these twelve years.

During this change, a new and assorted literature took shape. The new literature deeply penetrated the people's souls, and many intellectuals who felt committed thought they could promote freedom by joining political groups and parties. This was so important that even those who were well known for their pessimistic sentiments such as Sadiq Hedayat, Mohammad Masood and Bozorg Alavi abandoned their seclusion[76].

Anti-fascism feelings started emerging at that time. In the meantime, the Soviet socialist might, with its charming rhetoric, had, to some degree, attracted various intellectuals. Henceforth, authors like Jalal-Al-e-Ahmad and Syed Mohammad Ali Jamalzadeh represented the workers and peasantry as influential human elements in social changes in their respective stories. Saeed Nafisi, who wrote the Half Way to Paradise novel as a political treatise, uncovered numerous exceptional political figures amid Reza Shah's period. Also, in his book, The Flowers That Grew in Hell, published in 1953, he tried to pull the leg of all the cleric class and the administrative officials of Reza Shah by challenging their authoritarian rule.

[75.] Amir Naseer Katozian, 1993, p. 200).
[76.] Abedini, 1987, p.85رضا عابدینی در کتاب تاریخ طراحی

The nearly twenty years of Reza Shah's reign, from his rise to power in 1925 to his forced resignation in 1941, was a genuinely uneventful period in Persian literature, with the exception of the appearance of early instances of free verse. Following the example of Atatürk in Turkey, Reza Shah left on a general modernisation of his nation. He himself turned into a main force in launching the country into the modern age of reforms. On the other hand, Reza Shah's dictatorial and ruthless rule stifled all vestiges of the dearly-won freedom of expression and democracy. Politically motivated poetry, satire and journalism that were found in the works of 'Eshqi, Gilani, Farrokhi, Qazvini, Lahuti and Iraj Mirza' disappeared, and freedom of expression declined forcefully. Poets either dedicated themselves to thoughtful and philosophical subjects, or they alluded to social grievances in dubious and metaphorical ways. Political verse satire, which had been such an outstanding feature of an earlier age, became something of the past, and only criticism of a very general nature was endured. Before the end of Reza Shah's reign, of the six abovementioned poets, 'Eshqi was assassinated, Farrokhi perished in prison, Lahuti fled to Russia, Gilani died in a lunatic asylum, where he was forcibly confined, and the other two died of natural causes. Assassinations were an integral part of Reza Shah's reign[77].

Classical writers presented their thoughts through their works, but Bahar and Parvin Etesami were the most outstanding classical poets of that time. Parvin Etesami, the daughter of the well-known journalist and poet Yosuf Etesami, had a modern education at the American Girls' College in Tehran and was well-trained in classical poetry.

Although almost untouched by the turbulent years of the early twentieth-century in Iran and their politics, she was one of the country's most talented and influential poetesses. Imitating the art and the languages of the great masters, she wrote *ghazals*, *qasidehs* and poetical dialogues (*munaziras*) in the classical style but with the philosophical and moral themes of modern times. Parvin Etesami had great sympathy for the misery and suffering of the poor and also for the plight of women. According to Rypka, her themes and subject matter were extremely novel:

[77] Jamalzadeh, Muhammad Ali, 1339 جمالزاده. یکی بودویکی نبود. برلین. چاپخانه کاویانی

She hardly grazed the surface of the really urgent problems, even in the poems on social themes. She did not attempt to find a solution or to penetrate deeply into the social context but lapsed into sentimental and affected melancholy[78].

This has been discussed in Iran, and if she had lived longer, she would surely have reached greater heights in Persian poetry. Other prominent writers were Mohammad Hussain Shahryar and Rahi Mo'ayyeri. They were the traditional poets of recent times. While last was, for the most part, known for his ghazals (*Sayeh-e-omr* [Shadow of Life], 1954), the former wrote in a variety of traditional forms and even tried his hand at free verse. He honed a similar variance in his political life, easily abandoning the Pahlavis to sing the praises of the Islamic revolution. His "*Ai waa-ye- Madaram*" (Oh My Mother) and "*Payam be Einstein*" (A Message to Einstein) are two exceptional examples of his blank verse. In lyrical poetry, Shahryar's *ghazals* are in the style of Sa'di and Hafez. He depicted the style of the seventh-century writers in modern times by targeting the social causes of Iran.

Mohammad Hussain Shahryar broke new ground by writing poetry in his native Azerbaijani Turkish, which was frowned upon under the Pahlavi reign.

f) The Rule of Breaking Traditions: New Poetry (*She's-e Now*):-

While the formal and traditional type of sort of verse proceeded in Persian, from the second decade of the twentieth-century, writers tried different things with modern poetry and blank verse. Shams Kasmai, Taqi Ra'fat and Ja'far Khamene'i, some under French and others under Turkish literary influence, tried their hand at new forms and styles. It was Nima Yushij who changed the course of Persian verse. He lived a modest and simple life between his native village in the mountains of Mazandaran and Tehran and never travelled abroad. He knew French, and the influence of the French Impressionists was instrumental for him. He decided to put Persian poetry on a new route in the manifesto of his 'poetic ideology', which he hypothesised for the first time at the first Congress of Persian Writers in 1946, where he announced his departure from the old classical prosody

---

[78.] Rypka, Jan, History of Iranian Literature, Dordrecht 1968.

(*aruz*) and his adoption of a new style "*sher-e-azad*" (free verse) that had not been used previously[79].

g) Fiction in Modern Persian Literature: -

There were so many authors during the constitutional movements that Mirza Mohammad Baqer Khosravi was one of the prominent writers who, like many other intellectuals of his time, joined the constitutional movement. During the struggle with the forces of Mohammad Ali Shah, Khosravi retired to his native Kermanshah. The most outstanding among his novels are a trilogy entitled *Shams va toghra* (Sun and Sign), *Mari-ye Venizi* (Mary of Venice) and *Toghrol va Homa*. In essence, they are three romantic novels in which historical details are not treated convincingly, but it has been claimed that these novels played a marvellous role by depicting the socio-political conditions of Iran and the Pahlavi dynasty[80].

Syed Mohammad Ali Jamalzadeh's "*Yeki bud ye ki nabud*" (Once-Upon-a-Time) was published in the year 1921 in the journal called *Kaveh* from Berlin. This work of Jamalzadeh changed the perception of short story writing not only in Persian but in Persian fiction as well. Apart from utilising the techniques of the modern short story in this collection, in his interesting introduction to the volume, Jamalzadeh fervently condemns the traditionalists in Persian writing who write for the learned few and ignore the general public by using unrealistic and fancy language. Earlier, Dehkhoda, in his satirical writing named *Charand-va-parand*, had made very real use of colloquial and expressive language, but Jamalzadeh, in his short stories, proved better than him. Though contemporary with other writers such as Jahangir Jalili, Mohammad Masud (who was assassinated in 1947), Ali Dashti and Mohammad Hejazi, Jamalzadeh is considered the father of Persian fiction. He supported a simplification of the literary language and invited writers to use a style that was closer to colloquial speech in Iran. He used idioms and expressions of everyday life and opened a new chapter in Persian prose. Later on, it was seen in the works of Sadeq

---

[79] H. Kamshad, Modern Persian Prose Literature, Cambridge 1966.
[80] Ahmad, Kasravi, Tarikh-e Mashruted-ye Iran (History of the Iranian Constitutional Revolution), in Persian, Negah Publications, Tehran, 2003, Note; This book is also available in two volumes, published by Amir Kabir Publications In 1984.

Hedayat that the new style reached perfection and became a model for the younger generations of Persian writers.

One of the imminent writers with absolute talent was Sadeq Hedayat, who is perhaps the most well-known Iranian author. Subsequent to being taught in Europe, he came back to Tehran in 1930 and published a series of brilliant short stories, like Zindeh beh gur (Buried Alive), Seh qatreh khun (Three Drops of Blood), Vagh sahab (Mr Bow-Wow), Sag-e- velgard (The Stray Dog), and a longer story called Allaviyeh khanom. In all these works, Hedayat depicts, with remarkable sensitivity, insight and understanding, the lives, aspirations, anxieties and sorrows of his characters. His most famous and controversial novel is *Buf-e kur* (The Blind Owl), which has been translated into English and many other European languages. Its miserable and Kafkaesque world is very different from the atmosphere of his other works of fiction. Sadeq Hedayat's satirical works of fiction are *Tup-e-morvarid* and *Haji agha*. The previous is a severe satire on the despotic rule of Reza Shah and the beliefs and practices of Islam. The latter is a satire on the life of a hypocritical miser who changes himself like a chameleon in his political ideologies in order to suit the occasion. He targets the political class at large, who generally think that the people of Iran have no life to live with their dignity[81].

---

[81] Manoocher Aryanpur and M. Azādeh, A Short View of Modern Persian Literature, Books Abroad, Vol. 46, No. 2, pp. 200-210, 1972.

Analytical Approach of Modernist Writers Who Influenced the Iranian Revolution 1979

a) The Writers Who Left Their Impact to Influence the Revolution:-

Traditionally, Persian prose was a medium for dispensing historical, philosophical and scientific knowledge, sometimes in the guise of autobiographies. The novel and short story were rarely used, and it was chiefly in poetry that emotional expression was found. During the sixteenth to eighteenth centuries, the Persian prose style was both obscure and flowery in nature, and it reflected the formalised society of which the writers were a part. At the beginning of the nineteenth-century, increased cultural contact with Europe and social mobility created a desire for prose; this was strengthened by political movements, which later culminated in the Constitution of 1906. However, the forerunners of modern prose writers recognised the clumsiness of the existing prose forms. Thus, their first effort was a stylistic reform which sought to introduce a simple way of expression. The factors which contributed to this movement were: Travel books about Europe written by kings, princes, businessmen, and scholars, newspapers and journals, Translations of such European writers as Moliere and Dumas, Critical novels and plays such as Siyahatnameh Ibrahim Beig ("A Travel Book of Ibrahim Beig") by Z Maraghai and Mirza Malkom Khan's plays: Asharf Khan, Governor of Arabistana and Zaman Khan, Governor of Brujird, Historical novels such as Ishq va Saltanat ("Love and Kingdom") by Mussa Hamadani. These literary events were responsible for the further development of prose along three lines: conservative realism, social realism, and social individualism[82].

---

[82] For a discussion of twentieth-century Persian prose fiction, see Hassan Kamshad, Modern Persian Prose Literature (Cambridge: Cambridge University Press, 1966); and M. R. Ghanoonparvar, Prophets of Doom: Literature as a Socio-political Phenomenon in Modern Iran (Lanham, MD: University Press of America, 1984). On the development of modern Persian poetry, see Ahmad Karimi-Hakkak, Recasting Persian Poetry: Scenarios of Poetic Modernity in Iran (Salt Lake City: University of Utah Press, 1995). On Iranian drama, see M. R.

Conservative realism has resulted from the ideological influence of Western Europe, social realism has grown out of the impact of modern Soviet thinking, and finally, social individualism is the product of rich Persian classics and humanistic values. A good representative of conservative realism is Mohammad Hijazi, who wrote his first novel Homa in 1929, Parichehar in 1930, Andishe in 1940, and Aaiine ("Mirror") in 1954.

In all his works the author deals with the social events of urban life, and his characters are drawn from the middle class. Some are like Homa, a type of modern girl whom the author idealises. Such a girl is one who knows the rules of conduct, is modest and behaves in a way acceptable to a conservative liberal group. In contrast, Parichehr, although from the same middle class, rebels against traditional values. Aaiine, written twenty-five years after the first novel, is more comprehensive.

Ali Dashti belongs to the same literary school. More than any other modern writer, he desires to give a picture of modern Persian women. He selects his characters from the upper-class, usually Western-oriented, wealthy, and attractive people. His women are frequently the product of two cultures, and he presents them as wanting social equality without accepting social responsibility. Another writer who can be thought of as a link between conservative and social realism is the well-known critic Saeed Nafisi[83].

He was one of the first contributors to modern prose and has translated quite a number of French writings. He is equally at home in almost all literary media: press, short stories, and historical and social novels; among his works are Mah-e- Nakhshab ("Moon of Nakhshab"), Sitarigan Siya ("The Black Stars,") Farangis, and Nime Re Behisht ("Half Way to Paradise.") A representative of the literary school of social realism is Bozorg' Alavi, who wrote his first work in 1934. Influenced by Freud, he tries to interpret his characters in terms of Freudian psychology. During the Thirties, he was imprisoned, and when he was released in 1941, he published two books. In one of them, "Fifty-Three Persons," he discusses the life and treatment of this group of people while in prison. The second book, Varaq Parehaye

---

Ghanoonparvar and John Green, eds., Iranian Drama: An Anthology (Costa Mesa, CA: Mazda, 1989). James D. Clark's English translation of Siyahatnameh Ibrahim Beig was published as The Travel Diary of Ibrahim Beig (Costa Mesa, CA: Mazda, 2006).

[83.] Mohammad Ali Jazayery, Review; Modern Persian Prose Literature, Journal of the American Oriental Society.

Zindan ("The Torn Pages of Prison,") is again a description of his years in jail. In the collection is a masterful essay addressed to his wife and expressing his emotions just after receiving news of his release. Among his other works are Nameha ("Letters") Shirin, Dizashub, Ijareh ("Rent"), Zane Khoshbakht ("A Happy Woman") plus some translations of Chekhov. Jalal-Al-e-Ahmad is another writer of the social realist school. He takes his characters from the devoutly religious lower class and describes them sympathetically so as to reveal their mode of thinking. Among his early books is Ziyarat, which describes the adventures of a young man on a pilgrimage. Another of his works is a collection of stories called Did-va-Bazdid ("Visits") written in 1946 and based on social customs. "Az Ranji Ke ma Mi brim" ("The Pain That Makes Us Suffer") and Se Tar ("The Three Strings") were written in 1947. 'I atimadzade also belongs to this same group of writers.' In his writing, he tries to show different aspects of life, and in doing so, he criticises social conditions. For instance, the theme of Zivar is that money, regardless of the way in which it is acquired, has become the criterion of social prestige. Some of his other works are "Cat of Ramezan," Dokhtar-e-Ra'ayat ("The Villager's Daughter") and Kabutar-e-Solh ("Dove of Peace"). Sadiq Chubak is another social writer whose book Khayme Shab Bazi contains eleven sections, each one being a real picture of daily life. Like a painter, the writer selects his subjects well and portrays them with considerable skill. This also characterises the writing of Okhovat, whose story "Sib-e-Sorkh" ("The Red Apple") is told very simply to express the genuine emotional experiences of a maidservant. Tired of the insults and of the way she is treated by her master, she takes steps to end this kind of life. Undoubtedly, the cultural contact of the Iranian elite with both Western Europe and Russia has contributed somewhat to these writings, but in addition, the universal and humanistic quality of Persian classical poets has also been deeply ingrained in the minds of many modern Persian writers. These two sources, along with the element of nonconformity (an essential element of Persian culture), have produced writers who are professionally broad in scope but socially misfitted. A good representative of this group is Sadiq Hidayat, who is, perhaps, the greatest short story writer of modern Persian literature. His list of writings begins with "Zindeh-Be-gur" ("Half Dead") in 1902, followed by many others, among them: "Isfahan Nisfe Jahan" ("Isfahan- Half of the World"), "Sag-e-

Virlgard" ("Street Dog") and "Buf-e- Kur" ("The Blind Owl"). His stories total more than thirty[84].

Humanism and nationalism inspired him to investigate and describe various social groups. His kind heart took him into the life of the lower class, although he did not ignore other groups. He selected his characters and subjects with mastery and revealed their mode of life and mindset with great perceptive depth. This thorough understanding of the minds and emotions of people, plus his own deep sensitivity, gave him good reason to write. His works show both vertical and horizontal dimensions. He takes his readers to near and distant places at various times and introduces them to many groups of people who make up the world. He does not always write of the present but takes one to the wonders of the past, describes the adventures of early man, then takes him up the ladder of civilisation and dangles him hopelessly over an abyss. Not content with this, he directs him to the beautiful, and man becomes a perfectionist and makes a new mental world for himself; but soon, finding that the realm of metaphysics is unconvincing, he returns to this earthly world and grasps all its pain and evil. Finally, having tested all varieties of life, he withdraws into solitude. Not content with the short story and novel, Persian writers have resorted to other literary media. Many social critics have been masters of satire[85].

Ali Akbar Dehkoda, a writer in the early twentieth-century, was a skillful satirist, as was Sadiq Hedayat. Other recognised literary works are collections of folklore that were first begun by Hedayat. Many children's stories have also been gathered, the most famous of which are those of Sobhi Mohtadi. This brief analysis discloses that the progress of modern Persian prose has been more a result of political writing than of pure literary activity. Political unrest and a new evaluation of the place of man in society brought about special newspapers whose chief purpose was to awaken the people. It was necessary for writers to employ a simple style and direct their ideas toward public and national problems. Historians, translators and literary men were all involved in this movement. Inspiration came from European

---

[84] E. Yarshater, Ddstanhii-yi iriTn-i Bastan,Tehran, 1336/1957-58).

[85] Iranian Studies, Vol. 31, No. 3/4, A Review of the "Encyclopaedia Iranica" (Summer Autumn, 1998), pp. 543-559, Retrieved from JSTORE, http://www.jstor.org/stable/4311188.

countries and Persian culture itself. As a result, three literary movements emerged, as we have seen[86].

b) The Philosophy Behind the Artistic Style: -

The important question still remains: Can any of these groups be considered as a comprehensive literary school? This is not easy to answer, typically because modern prose has had little time to mature, and both international and domestic events have prevented Iran from developing a social philosophy which would give writers a sense of purpose. However, the elements of romanticism, sentimentalism, idealism, and especially realism are all evident in the works of modern prose writers. Still, they lack the social richness of a strong literary movement and do not penetrate deeply into social issues. Perhaps a more comprehensive prose requires more mature social conditions and freer ground.

There is no deficiency of narrative writers in traditional Persian writing. Traditional Persian writing in the latter part of the nineteenth-century, while expanding contacts with Europe, led to a reform of Persian prose and the adoption of new genres. The Persian translation of the picaresque exemplary Haji Baba of Isfahan and the presence of Abrahim Beig's Safar Nameh (Istanbul 1888, Calcutta 1890 and 1910) framed the vanguard of a rising flow of works written in prose. The various writers, notably Mohamad Bagher Khosravi (Shamso Toghra, 1909), Sheikh Mussa Nassry ("Love and Kingship," 1919), A. H. San'ati- Zadeh ("The Tale of Manes the Painter," 1927), Moshfegh Kazemi ("The Horrible Tehran," 1922), Abbas Khalili ("Secrets of Night," 1926), and Mohammad Mas'iid ("Night Entertainments," 1932) encouraged further expand the horizons of narrative prose. For Iran, as in different nations in a comparable phase of advancement - and for generally similar reasons- writing is steadily supplanting verse in numerous territories of creative and artistic expression[87].

The other perspective is the history of Persian narrative prose, which delighted in extraordinary fame in the fifties but whose efficiency and

---

[86] RYPKA, JAN, History of Iranian Literature, D. Reided Publishing Company Dordrecht- Holland- 1068.

[87] Aryanpur, Manoocher and M. Azādeh, Retrospect and Progress: A Short View of Modern Persian Literature: Reviewed work(s): Source: Books Abroad, Vol. 46, No. 2 (Spring, 1972), pp. 200-210

impact have been diminishing lately. The first of these is Ali Dashti, an adaptable man with a long and recognised profession as an author, researcher, negotiator, and representative. Dashti's better-known basic books are: "Hafez's Design," (1957), "Sadi's Domain" (1959), and "A While with Khayyam" (1965). In these, he consolidates a strong learning of Persian writing with western strategies for research and feedback. The outcome is a progression of books whose experiences are rendered more fitting through the writer's agile composition and clear creative ability. Dashti's creative notoriety, be that as it may, originates from his books, particularly Fetneh (1949); the universe of Ali Dashti's books needs to do with high society characters, sex, betting, and numerous exercises of the pseudo-savvy people of present-day Iran. His characters, for the most part, squander their lives in a soil of nostalgia, lachrymose sentiment, bad habit, triviality, and an aesthetic awareness, which at times goes past the facade of bona fide workmanship and culture. Dashti's defect is that he considers his own imaginary world excessively important and is generally incapable, making it impossible to rise above and condemn it with the unit of a craftsman who makes intentionally and to uncover and change. Dashti is no Anatole France. What reclaims his composition, regardless, is rich, familiar writing and a prolific creative imagination. More likely, the writer and his writings were somewhere stuck with the reality of contemporary Iran[88].

Meanwhile, Iran's more seasoned author and her most well-known writer is Mohammad Hejazi (1899), who for quite a long time was an administrative of the Ministry of Post and Telegraph and, as of late, a senator. Hejazi's tremendous output includes essays and translations as well as novels and short stories. Among his best known works is Homa (1927), the story of a girl who is in love with a youth but is herself a victim of the jealous love of her protector. The love triangle is resolved when the Russians take away the guardian. Hejazi's next novel, Parichehr (1929), depicts the vagaries of a loose woman's life. Ziba (1931) is a long novel (originally published in instalments) dealing with the life of a beautiful and influential woman and a young man of modest means who, getting entrapped by her affection, is drawn into her universe of bad habit and corruption. Parvana and Sereshk, both distributed in the fifties, resemble Hejazi's different books and novels

---

[88.] Kamshad, Hasan Modern Persian Prose Literature, Cambridge University press 1966.

in style and subject matter. The first, for instance, is about a young lady who relates with a youthful author and begins to look all starry-eyed at him without having seen him. The far-fetched sentiment closes with the young lady's suicide, and the author takes steps to spurn human love for profound. The whole work itself is a depiction of the exact society where the norms of the society talk about practicality more[89].

Mohammad Hejazi (like Dashti) is, for the most part, worried about sentiment and the issues of domestic life and seems virtually unaffected by the great social and political issues of his time. His tendency toward sentiment, a most despicable aspect of numerous contemporary Persian writers and explicit didacticism, and his frequent powerlessness to make believable characters and situations all detract from the artistic worth of his writings. On the positive side is Hejazi's familiar fluent, well-polished prose, a righteousness which has made his work a model of sound, effective writing in modern Persian literature[90].

The other prominent Iranian writer is Borzorg Alavi (1907), whose composition has been unfavourably influenced by his political perspectives. Subsequent to getting his initial training in Iran, he went to Germany for higher study. There, he adjusted himself to a gathering of Persian students with communist leanings. In 1937, soon after his return to Iran, Bozorg Alavi and fifty-two others were arrested as communists. Discharged from imprisonment in 1941, he started a time of participation with the socialist Tudeh Party, which kept going until the fall of Mossaddaq and the abuse of communists. Bozorg Alavi's works incorporate three accumulations of papers and short stories: "Bag" (1934), "Torn Sheets from Prison" (1941) and "Letters" (1952). He has additionally written a novel entitled "Her Eyes" (1952). This is about the education, love, and revolutionary activities of a rich, spoiled, and beautiful girl named Farangis. The book is not allowed in Iran. It has been criticised even in socialist circles outside Iran on ideological grounds. However, ideology aside, Alavi's work is exceptional not just in light of his sharp knowledge of the financial and psychological roots of human inspiration but also because of his sinewy and precise prose, in addition to his strong and exact exposition. Nonetheless, Bozorg Alavi

---

[89]. Homa Katuzian, Sadeq Hedayat, the Life and Legend of an Iranian Writer, London and New York 1991
[90]. Ibid

is one of the founders of an extensive number of promising Iranian writers whose either financial or political contemplations have crashed into virtual creative retirement[91].

Among the many writers in the field of modern Persian prose two, Sadiq Hedayat (1903-51) and Syed Md Ali Jamalzadeh (1895-71), emerge both for the nature of their work and the significant impact they have had on younger writers as significant. Both of them studied abroad; both were influenced by European (especially French) literary conventions, and, above all, both wrote in a style that reflected the naturalness of spoken language and was free of the burdening formality and over-ornamentations of their ancestors. Their works constitute the main significant endeavours toward making another ethos in Persian narrative literature and toward attuning the language to the demands of our times. Therefore, the work of these two writers, particularly Jamalzadeh's "Once-Upon-a-Time" (1921) and Hedayat's "Blind Owl" (1937), has already attained the position of classics in modern Persian writings. Considerations of space and the way that this short overview is restricted to living creators prohibit a fuller discussion of Jamalzadeh and Hedayat. It would be no real exaggeration to state, however, that their influence on Persian prose narrative is comparable to any other writers from European countries[92].

Among Hedayat's prior and more outstanding followers is Jalal-Al-Ahmad, the creator of "The Visit" (1945), "From the Pain We Suffer" (1947), "Undesirable Woman" (1952), and "The Principal" (1958). His most recent book, much discussed however inaccessible in Iran, is Gharzedeghi, a work in which he censures the submissive impersonation of the West. Another imperative adherent of Hedayat is Sadiq Chubak, the creator of the renowned short story gathering and of the lesser-known "The Chimp Whose Trainer Had Died," Tangsir, and Sang-e Sabur. Chubak is a consummate artist whose naturalistic approach and carefulness have empowered him to make distinctive pictures of life in contemporary Iran[93].

---

[91] Manoocher Aryanpur and M. Azādeh, A Short View of Modern Persian Literature, Vol. 46, No. 2 (Spring, 1972), pp. 200-210 Board of Regents of the University of Oklahoma http://www.jstor.org/stable/40126072 Retrieved from JSTORE.

[92] روزبه، محمد رضا، ادبيات معاصر ايران (نثر)، نشرروزگار تهران، 1388ش

[93] Chubak, Sadegh, Sang-i-sabur, Shirkat-i- Kitab, Los angles, 1369.

Over the most recent couple of years, an impressive number of new writers have appeared on the literary scene. Best known amongst these are Beh Azin, the author of "Farmer's Daughter," Taghi Modarresy, the writer of Yakulyd, and Mohammad Ali Afghani, the author of "Ahu Khanom's Husband." The last mentioned is a long novel about a shopkeeper who, though married for many years to Ahu Khanom, experiences passionate feelings with an enchantress named Homa and loses his peace of mind and decency in order to gain her. It is considered to be the most prevalent novel of the decade. "Ahu Khanom's Husband" offers the reader an engrossing plot and, in addition, an abundance of characters and scenes reflecting contemporary Iran. It is this wealth that has already prompted some of Afghani's avid admirers to compare him with Leo Tolstoy. Another writer, Hakimfar, has appeared in his books that he is skilled with phenomenal ability. However, the meagre income derived from writing Persian books has forced him (as it has many other writers) into literary dormancy[94].

c) Jamalzadeh and Sadlq Hedayt's Depiction: -

By a wide margin, the most proliferous genre in modern Persian literature is short stories. Following the case of Sadiq Hedayat and Syed Md Ali Jamalzadeh, Persian writers show a marked preference for depicting the life and idiom of the common people, for the old as opposed to the new, the poor as opposed to the rich. What's more, there is much enthusiasm for reflecting those aspects of life customs, beliefs, and linguistic peculiarities-which are most threatened by modernism and industrialisation[95].

There were some other younger writers, like Moradi Kermani (Masumeh, 1971), whose work enjoys popularity and may, in the future, enter the records of Persian literary history. On account of their commitments, Persian prose is detaching remnants of its post-Timurid system of verbosity, Arabism, and over-ornamentation and is adding new dimensions to its expressive forces. A look at what is right on sale at the bookstores of Tehran can give an idea of the volume and decent variety of prose being produced in Iran today. A decent number of these are written in a straightforward, supple style that

---

[94] Kamshad, Hasan Modern Persian Prose Literature, Cambridge University press 1966.

[95] Muhammad Kasimzadeh Modern Iranian writers. Tehran 2004, محمد قاسم زاده . داستان نویسان معاصر ایران. تهران 2004

makes those of early compositions and prose reformists look outdated and firm by contrast. The whole idea was established by the writers to bring the social scenario in one frame so that one could see the progressive approach of the various narrations.

Here are two examples taken from two late accumulations of short stories:

"The breeze was a meandering minstrel of the forsake. It goes by towns and talks with poplars. A solitary ring dove is looking for his mate. Do you not see his body among your branches?"

(Nader Ibrahimi, "A Dwelling for the Night")

"Amid the evening, the deadlock back street of Lotf Ali Khan resembled a subterranean insect gap in which water had been poured." Around sixty or seventy offspring of various ages with canvas pants, exposed feet, pale faces, and scars would immerse the rear way. Some would assemble bonfires with old newspapers and rags. Some would bring water in tin jars and fabricate mud houses. The more established ones would nail a string over the back road and play volleyball. In short, all year long, Lotf Ali Khan's alley was a veritable zoo in the evenings[96].

d) The modern Persian Poetry and its impact: -

Modern Persian poetry had to play a very vital role. It has had to contend against one major obstruction: the mutual resentment of traditionalists and modernists. In prose, partly because of the obvious decadence of the older styles and partly because of the pressing need for a more practical style to answer the needs of a developing society, the change of Persian writing accepted the power of an idea whose time had come. However, in the case of poetry, the situation was quite different from that of prose. The so-called Return Movement, which started under the Safavids, brought about a restoration of conventional verse. Emulating the manner of poets like Rudaki and Ferdowsi, the writing of qasidehs and other traditional forms and succeeded in stating modern sensibilities, communicating present-day sensibilities through traditional symbolism and expression. The work

---

[96] Homa Katuzian, Sadeq Hedayat, the Life and Legend of an Iranian Writer, London and New York 1991.

of such poets as Arif Qazvini (1882-1934), Iraj Mirza (1874-1924), and especially Taqi Bahar (1886-1951) turned out to be massively well-known and showed that traditional forms can still serve for the expression of the most complex and delicate of modern thoughts. Thus, from the very start, there was a firm resistance against the individuals who, like Nima Yushij, got rid of conventional metres and stanzas and tried different things with more up-to-date frames. This restriction is as significant and has led to occasional acrimony and created a dichotomy among poets according to their metrical loyalties. There are authors of verse (sher) and writers of "new" poetry (sher-e-nov). Few anthologies include poems from both groups of that time[97].

Among traditional writers, Abul Qasim Lahuti (1887-1957) and Bahar are notable for the exceptional merit of some of their poems. Following the example of Bahar, they have tried, with impressive results, to adapt the old forms to the demands of the modern world. Two of the most prolific and popular of traditional poets are Rahi Moayeri and Mohammad Hussain Shahriyar. Moayeri's works, particularly his stories and his love poems, are portrayed by streaming lines and a mix of education, humour, and sentiment, which recalls Sadi's lighter poems. His mind is best represented in such epigrammatic lyrics as the following:

A poet once complained to a sage

Of a cruel thief's terrible outrage

I had written jewels in prose and verse, said he,

The thief stole all my work! Every page!

Moaned the poet: "Alas the day, woe is me."

"I pity the thief," replied the sage[98]

This poetry is indirectly targeting the regime of contemporary Iran, where the people were brutalised by the anarchy system.

---

[97] Hasan Mirabidini. Centenary of Iranian prose. 1st and 2nd volumes. Revised edition, Tehran. حسن میر عابدینی صدسالداتان2004.

[98] LahutiI, Abul-Qasim, A prominent writer whose contribution can not be forgotten and the discussion retrieved from the given link here: http://www.iranicaonline.org/articles/lahuti-abul-qasem.

Mohammad Hossein Shahriar's poetry has an ardency, intensity, and metrical smoothness unmatched by any other contemporary writer. He is not an innovator either in metrics or diction; his contribution- and one of the causes of his popularity- is his ability to turn older moulds, particularly those of Hafez, into poetry that is at once moving and exceptionally well-wrought. This enthusiastic writer started by creating a sad verse. Huge numbers of his self-contradicting recollections are reflected in his books Hazyan-e-Del, Heydar Baba, and Mumiyai. Heydar Baba, formed in Turkish and later converted into Persian, was for quite a while on 'the main ten smash hit list in Tehran,' Heydar Baba is the name of a mountain where the writer spent his youth. He additionally composed a book of epic lyrics, Takht-e Jamshid.

Nima Yushij (Ali Esfandiary, 1896-1959) is the recognised pioneer of Sher-e Nov in Iran. Conceived in the Noor region of Mazandaran, he got his training there and later in Tehran, where he mastered the French language and learned about the work of European poets. It was this information that fortified his own particular thoughts regarding the advancement of Persian verse and prompted the definition of his proposals for she'r-e nov. Subsequently, in 1921, he drew out his first accumulation of she'r-e nov entitled Afsaneh. From that point onward, Nima composed numerous books of poetry as well as pieces on the reform of Persian prosody. The substance of his thoughts regarding poetry was given in a lecture delivered at the First Congress of Writers held in 1946. A piece of it goes this way: "In my free verse, rhythm and rhyme are taken in an unexpected way." In them, the shortening or extending of hemistichs did not depend on impulse. I put stock all together, even in disorder lines. Each of my phrases joins the others according to a framework. For me, it is more difficult to make free verse than the other kind. The principal element of my poetry is my suffering. As I see it, there is no evidence that the writer can be without this fixing. To me, form, diction, rhythm, and rhyme have always been tools which I have had to modify so as to make them better suited to convey my sufferings and that of others. Nima Yushij is a writer who writes in a very simple language which likens the woods and mountains.

Nima Yushij writings cover many subjects, but his best poems are usually those in which a description of nature leads to considerations of such problems as life and death. His love poems are also of unusual charm.

The following is a translation of one of his shorter poems called "Dar Kenar-e-Rudkhaneh" (On the River Bank),

On the river bank dawdles the boulder, ancient of the spine.

The day it's a sunny day.

The scene of her coming is warm,

Ancient, ask sin sun's warm lap, soundly sleeps,

On the riverbank

On the same river bank, I stand alone,

Weary of the pain of longing,

Expecting my sun;

My eyes, though,

Find her not.

My sun

Has taken her face to far-away waters

Sunlit is everything everywhere,

But because of my delay

Or my haste

Only my sun is absent

On the riverbank[99]

It is hard to overestimate the influence of Nima Yushij on the development of sher-e nov. His writings have inspired a large group of younger writers to try new departures.

---

[99] Manoocher Aryanpur and M.Azadeh, A Short View of Modern Persian Literature, Vol. 46, No. 2 (Spring, 1972), pp. 200-210 Board of Regents of the University of Oklahoma http://www.jstor.org/stable/40126072 Retrieved from JSTORE.

One of his best writings can also be seen in the following poetry below:

My House Is Cloudy

My house is overcast by clouds

Permanently weighed by a pall of cloud over the earth.

The wind, broken, desolate and intoxicated,

Whirls over the pass.

The world is laid waste by it

And my senses, too!

O piper!

O you enchanted by the music of the pipe, where are you?

My house is cloudy, yet

The cloud is impregnated by rain.

Cherished by the illusion of my bright days,

I stand opposite the sun

I cast my gaze upon the sea.

And the entire world is desolated and ravaged by the wind

And the ever-playing piper progresses onto his path

In this cloudy world[100].

(Translation of Nima Yushij work by Ali Salami)

Besides, Nima Yushij improved his pictures with personifications that were altogether different from the "frozen" imagery of the moon, the rose garden, and the tavern. His unconventional poetic diction took poetry out of the

---

[100]. This Poem is taken from the given link, which was also discussed by Ali Salami with the same link http://iranianarchives.org/poetry/nima-yushij/169-my-house-is-cloudy-by-nima-yushij, Retrieved from online education site.

rituals of the court and placed it squarely among the masses. The common discourse of the masses essentially added neighbourhood shading and flavour to his pieces. Ultimately, and by far, Nima Yushij's most emotional component was the use of symbolism. It has been believed that the Persian writers, with their respective literature, are the jewel in the crown of Persian culture, but still, it has failed to achieve or get the place it actually deserves.

Conclusion;

In conclusion, the significance of the modernist trend could be underlined, and the turning point moment in this direction could be the Islamic insurgency that triggered the improvement of Iranian literature and drew a clear-cut line between the literature before and after 1979. The difference could be observed during the periods in the quality and amount of art in the literary works, particularly in the prose. The pre-revolution literature, mainly prose, was focused on the socio, political and cultural aspects of Iran, but the post-revolution literature became multidimensional both in style and in thematic assortment, with additional positive ways to deal with the social life, mainly the marginalised section became and started showing active participation in every field. The short stories were written mainly to address the children, but the meaning was very much sarcastic. The short stories for children are viewed as a positive change; the literature about children and childhood memories is halfway raised on the grounds that it could fill a platform for some authors who contradicted ideological restrictions and chose it to express their way of protesting the youngsters' tongue. It was the time when advanced information technology was introduced, and communications meant a lot to them. Political stands to separate the Iranian culture rehearsing Islamic esteems did not increase support. Literature approached the foreign literary trend, and the pattern was managed to achieve the writers inside Iran and advanced Iranian literary activities. It was the time when humankind encountered the idea of globalisation, which represented a move towards socio-political, economic, and cultural proximity and conformity. Literature was picked up from the process of the worldwide exchange of thoughts between countries, and neighbourhood achievements were adopted universally. What is more, on account of its quality and distinct voice, the Iranian literature figured out how to pick up its due place in the world literature arena. This was conceivable in view of the hard expression of the capable writers who kept on experimenting, stimulating the established societies, and learning from the Persian classics and their contemporaries. Those days, it could be observed that in the short stories of contemporary writers, a person is delineated not as a mere demographic unity but as an individual with spiritual, traditional values who has an emotional way of conflicting needs and priorities. What is more, it is the prevailing method for looking at each character among contemporary Iranian writers. They additionally attempt to enter into the truth that influences the person to act the way he does, utilising new methods of portrayal and expanding the range and interest of the work. The procedure by which distinctive characters have been literally treated, depicted, and evolved can apply to the development of Iranian prose as a whole. The short stories and the modernist trend in Iran have become more advanced and mature. After a lot of intervention and presentation changes in the modernist trend and Persian literature during the nineteenth-century and the early moves towards the simplifications of the modern Persian prose style, it examines the adoption of new genres and styles under western techniques used by the writers. The intention towards using colloquialism, the treatment of political and social issues, and the advancement of these trends have been up to recent times. The set writing styles were chosen from a range of imaginary literature in the form of short stories. These days, authors have somehow tried to extract from novels, short stories, articles, and other social and political scenarios to present them in that form. The introduction was made to look upon the overview of thematic and expressive changes in Persian prose and poetry in the early ages of the twentieth-century, mainly the constitutional movement around 1905-11. The modernist trend in Persian literature was then viewed through the study of the works by more conspicuous Iranian authors during the ages between 1920 and 1979. This was the time when secular patriotism evolved from 1921 to 1941. The early post-war was very much crucial in the sense that the writers of that time were followed up largely by the masses of Iran, and these prominent writers were mainly Syed Md Ali Jamalzadeh, Sadique Hedayat, Jalal-al- Ahmad and Simin Daneshwar. They were the writers of the common people of Iran who tried to express their thoughts while considering the Iranian situation at that time.

During the early ages of the nineteenth century, contacts between Europe and Iran quickly expanded. However, the war between Iran and Russia weakened the bounding. It is said that among the progressive members of the Qajar dynasty, changes in the Iranian culture and society were deeply felt or needed. The prompt efforts undertaken turned Iran towards the modernization of society. The aim was to establish and strengthen the relationship between their foreign advisers and cultural training. Precisely, it was meant to set up specialized enhancements.

The major considerations were the education of the new (modern) style and the culture of the European style. The role of the printing press became more important during the constitutional movements. Where there had been no press since the seventeenth century. The aim of that press was to enhance the proficiency of the government and the spread of information, and an attempt was made to simplify the written language as it was utilized by the authorities only. The young generation was sent abroad to study higher education and learn about cultural exchanges. They were expected that when they returned, they would know the new scientific and technical skills but also have knowledge of the Western education system. This was the time when Amir Kabir established the institution called Darul Fonun in Tehran, which was considered the first modern academic institution in Iran. Iran's political scenario could be understood by reading the ideas of Abdul Rahim Talibuf and Zainul Abedin. They were the ones who penetrated the idea of change. Their knowledge of the politics and social conditions of Iran forced them to prepare the minds of Iranians for political and social changes. This was the time in 1906 when the Constitution and Parliament were being instituted. Mohammad Taqi Bahar and Ali Akbar Dehkhoda were the writers who were very influential satirists of daily events and started the trend, which was known as a modernist trend in Persian literature.

During the reign of Reza Shah Pahlavi, freedom of expression was not allowed at all. However, the modernizing approaches of the administration were indirectly helpful in creating the settings for the development of new Persian literature. Nima Yushij was the first to propose a radical reinstatement of Persian poetry. Nima Yushij found the contradicting powers of tradition to be very strong. His sonnets were mainly influenced by French romanticism and symbolism. This was exactly the time when the writers from the modern era went on to set the trend called new poetry, "she-i-now", in Iran. Ahmad Shamlu, Forough Farrokhzad, Mehdi Akhwan Sales, and so many other writers were leading in modernizing the writing style. They were the ones who also distanced themselves from the classical, traditional Persian writing styles as well. Sohrab Sepahri set a new example by citing the mystical evocations of nature, which were very popular among Iranians. Their writing style in modern poetry was remarkable, as they also targeted social problems through their writings.

In the history of Persian literature, Syed Mohammad Ali Jamalzadeh (1892 – 1997) is considered the inaugurator of modern Persian prose fiction writer, and Nima Yushij (1897 – 1960) is considered the father of modern Persian poetry writer in the early twentieth century. It must be noted in mind that their works were preceded by the efforts of other fiction writers, poets, and playwrights in the late nineteenth century. When scholars look at the magnum opus of Ibrahim Beig, Siyahatnameh-ye-Ibrahim Beig (The Travel Memoirs of Ebrahim Beyg), a bridge between the dominant nineteenth-century prose genre of the safarnameh (travel memoirs) and twentieth-century fiction, as well as at the poetry of Mirzadeh Eshqi (and others) and the closet plays of Mirza Aqa Tabrizi before and during the Iranian constitutional revolution (1906 – 11), demonstrates that, in contrast to traditional Persian writing, the early modernists veered toward literature of social and political criticism. Jamalzadeh's stories became a landmark in the development of realistic prose narrative, where Sadique Hedayat tried in his magnum opus Buf-e-kur (The blind owl) to apply the common people's understanding and used the device of surrealism. Bozorg Alavi's "Chashmhayash" rightly pointed out in his writing the deeper causes of psychological problems and the experience of leftist' intellectuals in their struggles. Jalal Al-e-Ahmad's "Gharzadegi" (Westernization) had a great effect on the life of Iranians, which is a slavish imitation of the West under the Pahlavi Dynasty. Last but not least, while summing up, the contributions made by the women writers could not be forgotten in the history of Persian literature. Simin Dnishwar, Pravin Etsami and Forough Farrokhzad, through their poetry, became controversial because of their bold female voice and their harsh criticism of the position of women in Iranian society.

References

- Bahaqqui,Jafar Chun Sabu-ve-Tishna, University of Ferdowsi Iran 1135

- Kamshad, Hasan Modern Persian Prose Literature, Cambridge University press 1966

- Hakemi Ismail Adabiyat-e-Iran,Tehran

- Ishaque, Md SukhanwaraniNamii Iran, Ayada 1363

- Jamalzadeh, Muhammad Ali, Shaygan's Treasure, Berlin, 1916

- Jamalzadeh, Muhammad Ali, Iran and Russia Relations, Once-Upon-a-Time and Kaveh magazine, Berlin, 1921

- Jamalzadeh, Muhammad Ali, Prosperity Garden or Sadi's Counsels, Germany, 1938

- Jamalzadeh, Muhammad Ali, Lunatic Asylum and Story of Stories, Berlin, 1941

- Jamalzadeh, Muhammad Ali, Qoltashan Collection, Berlin 1946

- Jamalzadeh Muhammad Ali, Gathering Desert, Rah-AbNameh and A Man with Thousand Professions, Geneva, 1947

- Jamalzadeh,Muhammad Ali, Bitter and Sweet; translation of The Story of Mankind, Hendrik Wilhelm van Loon 1955

- Jamalzadeh, Muhammad Ali, Sar va Tah Yeh Karbas; translation of Wilhelm Tell and Don Carlos, Friedrich Schiller 1956

- Jamalzadeh, Muhammad Ali, Masterpiece Collections, 1958

- Jamalzadeh, Muhammad Ali, Old and New; translation of Democracy and Human Prestige 1959

- Jamalzadeh, Muhammad Ali, Acquaintance with Hafiz Thesis, Geneva 1988

- Jamalzadeh, Muhammad Ali,Talkh v Sheerin,Geneva,1955

- Jamalzadeh, Muhammad Ali Jamalzadeh, Kissahaiy-e-Kutah Braiye Bacchhaiy-e-Rishdaar, Geneve,1973

- Jamalzadeh, Muhammad Ali,Kisse Ma Be Sar Rasad,Geneva,1978

- Jamalzadeh, Muhammad Ali Jamalzadeh, Gair Az Khuda Hichkas Nabud, Fredrich,1941

- Jamalzadeh, Muhammad Ali,Asman Risman,Berlin,1964

- YahaiyaAryanpur, AzSaba t Nima (2), Tehran 1372

- YaqubAzand, Tarikh-i-AdabiyatNavin Iran, Tehran 1266

- Mohammad Ali Jazayery, Review; Modern Persian Prose Literature, Journal of the American Oriental Society,

- Jamalzadeh, Mohammad Ali, Encyclopedia Britannica online; www. iranicaonline.org/articles/jamalzadeh

- History of Iran, constitutional revolution 1906-1911, Iran Chamber Society, Tehran

- John Foran, The Strengths and Weaknesses of Iran's Populist Alliance; A Class Analysis of the constitutional revolution of 1905-1911, Theory and Society, Vol.20, No.6, pp. 795-823 (December 1991). JSTOR

- Nikki T. Keddie, with a section by Yann Richard, Modern Iran – Roots and Results of Revolution, updated edition (Yale University Press, New Haven, 2003).

- Ahmad, Kasravi, Tarikh-e Mashruted-ye Iran (History of the Iranian constitutional revolution), in Persian, Negah Publications, Tehran, 2003, Note; This book is also available in two volumes, published by Amir Kabir Publications In 1984.

- Ahmad, Kasravi, History of the Iranian constitutional revolution; Tarikh- Mashrute-ye Iran, Volume I, translated into English by Evan Siegel, Mazda Publications, Costa Mesa, California,2006

- RYPKA, JAN, History of Iranian Literature, D. Reided Publishing Company Dordrecht- Holland- 1068.

- Jamalzadeh Mohammad Ali; *Once-Upon-a-Time (Yeki Bud va Yeki Nabud) Heshmat* Moayyad; Paul Sprachman, Review by: Michael Craig Hillmann Journal of Near Eastern Studies, Vol. 47, No. 4 (Oct., 1988), pp. 311-313.

- Aryanpur, Manoocher and M. Azādeh, *Retrospect and Progress: A Short View of Modern Persian Literature*: Reviewed work(s): Source: Books Abroad, Vol. 46, No. 2 (Spring, 1972), pp. 200-210

- Al e Ahmad. Jalal, *Did-va-Bazdid*, Majmua I Dastan, Entessarat-e Amirkabir, Tehran 1979.

- Al e Ahmad. Jalal, *Gharbzadeghi*, Anjuman-e- Islami Iran, Tehran 1964

- Alavi. Bozorg, *Chamedan*, Tehran 1934.

- Alavi. Bozorg, *Panjah O Si Nafar*, Tehran 1988.

- Alavi. Bozorg, *Varaq Par haye zindan*, Tehran 1978.

- Chubak, Sadegh, *Sang-i-sabur*, Shirkat-i- Kitab, Los angles, 1369 (1990).

- Chubak.Sadegh, *Khemah Shab Bazi*, Shirkat-i- Kitab, Los angles, 1369 (1990).

- Hedayat, Sadique, *Sag-i- Vilgard*, Entessarat-e- Amirkabir, Tehran 1342(1963).

- Hedayat,Sadique, *Buf-e- kur*, Nasir-i- simurg, Tehran 1372(1993).

- Hedayat. Sadique, *Zinda Bi- gur*, Muassasa-i- Matbuati Amirkabir, Tehran 1958.

- Hedayat. Sadique, *Insan u Hayvan*,Nashr-e- Chashma, Tehran 1381(2002-03).

- Hedayat. Sadique, *Sa Qatrah Khoon*, Entessarat-e Amirkabir, Tehran 1341(1962).

- Chubak, Sadegh, *Sang-i-sabur*, Shirkat-i- Kitab, Los angles, 1369

➤ Chubak.Sadegh, *Khemah Shab Bazi*, Shirkat-i- Kitab, Los angles, 1369 (1990).

➤ Hedayat, Sadique, *Sag-i- Vilgard*, Entessarat-e- Amirkabir, Tehran 1342(1963).

➤ Hedayat,Sadique, *Buf-e- kur,* Nasir-i- simurg, Tehran 1372(1993).

➤ Hedayat. Sadique, *Zinda Bi- gur*, Muassasa-i- Matbuati Amirkabir, Tehran 1958.

➤ Hedayat. Sadique, *Insan u Hayvan,*Nashr-e- Chashma, Tehran 1381(2002-03).

➤ Hedayat. Sadique, *Sa Qatrah Khoon*, Entessarat-e Amirkabir, Tehran 1341(1962).

➤ Browne, E. G. The Persian Constitutional Movement, London: Milford, 1918.

➤ Browne, E. G.), A History of Persian Literature in Modern Times, Cambridge, Cambridge University Press,1924.

➤ Browne, E. G. A Year Among the Persians, Cambridge: Cambridge University, Press,1926.

➤ K. Chaykin. Concise essay on the modern Persian literature. M: 1928, pp. 144-145.

➤ Muhammad Huquqi. Overview: History of literature and modern Iranian literature. Tehran 1998.

Persian Reference

فارسی:

1. مرتضی راوندی. جلد اول، تاریخ اجتماعی ایران، 1353ق، تهران.

2. رضازاده شفق. تاریخ ادبیات ایران، 1969ق، آرمان.

3. جان ریپکا. تاریخ ادبیات و اجتماعی ایران، 1967

4. دیاکونوف میخائیل. تاریخ ایران باستان، (جلد دوم) 1380، (علمی و فرهنگی) تهران، ایران

5. دیاکونوف میخائیل. تاریخ ایران باستان، 1380، (علمی و فرهنگی) تهران، ایران

6. یعقوب آژند، انواع ادبی در ایران امروز، 1383 تهران

7. صفا ذبیح الله دکتر. تاریخ ادبیات در ایران، دانشگاه تهران، 1903 میلادی

8. یحیی آرین پور. از صبا تا نیما، جلد دوّم، تهران زوّار، 1372ش

9. از صبا تا نیما، جلد سوّم، تهران زوّار، 1372ش

10. سیّد محمد علی جمالزاده. یکی بود و یکی نبود، برلن، 1340ق

11. سیّد محمد علی جمالزاده. سرگزشته، تهران، 1336ق

12. سید محمد علی جمالزاده. تلخ و شیرین، تهران 1334ق

13. سید محمد علی جمالزاده. خلقیات ما ایرانیان، تهران، فروردین 1345ق

14. سید محمد علی جمالزاده. قلتشن دیوان، تهران 1325ق

15. جعفر یا حقی، چون سبوی تشنه، تهران 1375ق

16. یعقوب آژند. انواع ادبی در ایران امروز، تهران، 1383ق

17. حسن کامشاد. پایه گزاران نثر جدید فارسی، تهران، 1384ق

18. پرویز ناتل خانلری. هفتاد و دو سخن، فرهنگ و اجتماع، 1347ق

19. هاشمی، حمید، تاریخ ایران، کتاب خانه ملی ایران، تهران، 1331ش.

20. جمالزاده، محمد علی، سروته یک کرباس، انتشارات سخن، تهران، 1389ش.

21. جمالزاده، محمد علی، هزار بیشه، انتشارات سخن، تهران، 1384ش.

22. جمالزاده، محمد علی، آزادی و حیثیت انسانی، انتشارات سخن، تهران، 1384ش.

23. جمالزاده، محمد علی، خاطرات سید محمد علی جمالزاده، انتشارات سخن، تهران، 1380ش.

24. جمالزاده، محمد علی، فال و تماشا (مجموعهٔ مقالات ادبی)، انتشارات سخن، تهران، 1389ش.

25. جمالزاده، محمد علی، هفت کشور، انتشارات سخن، تهران، 1388ش.

26. جمالزاده، محمد علی، جنگ ترکمن، انتشارات سخن، تهران، 1386ش.

27. جمالزاده، محمد علی، تاریخ روابط روس و ایران انتشارات سخن، تهران، 1384ش.

28. جمالزاده، محمد علی، آسمان و ریسمان، انتشارات سخن، تهران، 1386ش.

29. جمالزاده، محمد علی، فرهنگ لغات عامیانه، انتشارات سخن، تهران، 1382ش.

30. جمالزاده، محمد علی، آشنایی با حافظ، انتشارات سخن، تهران، 1384ش.

31. جمالزاده، محمد علی، کهنه و نو، انتشارات سخن، تهران1388ش.

32. جمالزاده، محمد علی،داستان بشر انتشارات سخن، تهران، 1388ش.

33. جمالزاده، محمد علی، قصّه های کوتاه برای بچه های ریش دار، انتشارات سخن، تهران، 1389ش.

34. جمالزاده، محمد علی، نامه های ژنو(با همکاری محمد افشین وفایی، شهریار شاهین دژی)، انتشارات سخن، تهران، 1388ش.

35. جمالزاده، محمد علی، نامه های جمالزاده(درکتاب خانهٔ مرکزی دانشگاه تهران)، انتشارات سخن، تهران، 1387ش.

36. جمالزاده، محمد علی، برگزیدهٔ آثار، انتشارات سخن، تهران، 1389ش.

37. میر عابدینی، حسن، صد سال داستان نویسی ایران، جلد اوّل و دوّم، نشر چشمه، تهران، 1377ش.

38 میر عابدینی، حسن، صد سال داستان نویسی ایران، جلد سوّم و چهارم، نشر چشمه، تهران، 1387ش.

39 شکری، فدوی، واقعگرایی در ادبیات داستان معاصر، مؤسسه انتشارات نگاه، تهران 1386ش.

40 روزبه، محمد رضا، ادبیات معاصر ایران (نثر)، نشرروزگار ، تهران، 1388ش.

41 آرین پور، یحیی، از نیما تا روزگار ما (تاریخ ادب فارسی معاصر)، آماده سازی، چاپ شرکت قلم/چاپ خاشع، تهران 1384ش.

42 دست غیب، عبدالعلی، نقدِ آثارِ محمد علی جمالزاده، انتشارات چاپار، تهران، 1388.

43 مهرین، مهرداد، سرگزشت و کار جمالزاده، چاپ زهره، آذرماه، 1342ش.

44 احمد ظهور الدین، نیا ایرانی ادب، نگارشات میاں، لاهور، 2000م.